Eleanor's Diary

The Life of a Gentleman Farmer's Daughter 1804-5

The Diary of Eleanor Weatherly

Presented by Joan Wright

Eleanor's Diary; The Life of a Gentleman Farmer's Daughter – 1804-5

First published in the United Kingdom in 2014 by Wanney Books

www.wildsofwanney.co.uk

© 2014 Joan Wright

First paperback edition 2014

A catalogue record for this book is available from the British Library.

ISBN 978-0-9927324-1-7

Printed in the UK by Martins the Printers, Berwick-upon-Tweed

Although every precaution has been taken in the preparation of this book, the publisher and author assume no responsibility for errors or omissions. Neither is any liability assumed for damages resulting from the use of the information contained herein.

Wanney Books

wildsofwanney.co.uk

Contents

Acknowledgements

I am grateful to all those who have encouraged and supported me in this venture, without whom this book would not have been published.

My particular thanks are due to:

Elspeth Orrom for sharing the Diary with me; Jane Bowen for reading the manuscript and offering her thoughtful suggestions; Ian Hall for his interest and technical support; Philippa Craig for the loan of the Weatherly papers.

The Association of Northumberland Local History Societies and Belford & District Local History Society for funding.

Joan Wright

Belford

May 2014

Front cover picture: Maureen Burns

Pen and ink sketches: Anne Wright

Image credits

1; courtesy of John Sutherland

3, 5; reproduced with permission of Northumberland Archives

9; reproduced with permission of the Craster family

10, 12 and back cover; courtesy of Martin Orrom

11; courtesy of Philippa Craig

Introduction

A typed copy of a diary originally written in 1804 came to light in Belford in 2004. It had come from Cynthia Sanderson who once farmed at Newlands, just south of Belford. She in turn had been given it many years earlier by another farmer, Anthony Barber of Newham. His ancestors figured largely in the diary, as did some former tenants of Newlands. The journal had been written by Eleanor Weatherly, the 20 year old daughter of a gentleman farmer from Outchester.

1: An early photograph of Outchester House

This family were not native to the Belford area – the Weatherlys were mainly tenant farmers, scattered throughout Berwickshire. Eleanor's grandfather, James Weatherly, had farmed at Foulden Hill until his death in 1775. Her father, John, initially turned his back on the family tradition of farming; leasing a corn mill, he became a flour merchant and established a bakery business in Berwick. He married Mary, a daughter of Nicholas Whitehead, who came from a Northumberland family with links to Boulmer Hall since the 17th century. Their four children were born in Berwick – James, followed by Eleanor, Susan and finally Nicholas. Mary Weatherly died just days after their last child was born in December 1786.

Despite having a young family to rear, John Weatherly did not marry again. After the death of his young wife, he gave up his Berwick business and returned to his farming roots, taking a lease from the Royal Greenwich Hospital for Outchester farm near Belford.

His daughter Eleanor had been well educated, and competently schooled in the domestic skills of spinning, sewing and cooking. At the age of 20 she was confidently running the family household, and at the same time participating in an active social life across North Northumberland and the Scottish Borders.

It is evident from the diary that the family were well established there by 1804, and Eleanor and her sister had become good friends with Mary and Barbara, the daughters of John Dinning, the tenant at nearby Newlands.

2: Newlands today

Written just before the novels of Jane Austen were published, it is easy to identify with the period. But there the similarity ends. This is not a story about characters living in grand houses somewhere in 'Middle England', but an account of real families who lived in and around Belford. Here was an undiscovered piece of social history about the north of Northumberland, which had languished in a drawer for decades. Surely it deserved a wider audience?

Introduction

Although only a short distance from Belford, Outchester lies within the parish of Bamburgh. The Weatherly family were Presbyterians who normally worshipped at the Meeting House in Warenford, the only place of worship for dissenters in their parish. When it suited their purpose, however, the young siblings were not averse to making use of the pew of their friends in the parish church of St Mary in Belford.

At this time, except for a caretaker, Belford Hall was unoccupied, so with no resident squire it is rarely mentioned - the hub of social life was elsewhere. The Weatherly family and their acquaintances were of fairly comfortable means, and certainly believed in enjoying themselves – constantly travelling great distances in pursuit of company and entertainment.

For the young ladies, the subscription ball season was a much anticipated event; perhaps more usual entertainments were tea drinking or supper parties with dancing, together with race meetings and the theatre. In the winter months they and their friends played cards every day, and always for money. Indeed they were great gamblers and would place bets on just about anything. The favoured 'stake' for these bets was always a pair of gloves – which must have been music to the ears of the glove makers.

Many places and people frequent the pages of the diary and readers may find the maps, family tree and name glossary helpful.

Eleanor wrote phonetically and could be imaginative and erratic with spelling; for ease of reading the spelling has been standardised unless otherwise stated. The grammar is entirely her own!

3: Tickets for the Belford Subscription Ball

Eleanor's Northumberland

In the 17th century, Belford was described as a miserable place with a handful of wretched cottages; indeed even the church had only a small portion of the roof intact. Fortunately, thanks to the purchase of the Belford and Easington estate in 1726 by Abraham Dixon, a Newcastle merchant, and especially by the efforts of his enterprising son, another Abraham, all that was to change.

By 1804 Belford was a flourishing little post town. With a favourable position on the Great North Road, Dixon had the foresight to develop an excellent coaching inn, to be known as the Blue Bell. The Mail coach, started in 1786, ran between Edinburgh and Newcastle and due to demand, was followed in 1800 by the Union coach, a conveyance which could carry even more passengers – the fare to travel on the latter was sixpence per mile inside and four pence on top.

4: The Blue Bell Inn; Belford's Coaching Inn and scene of the subscription balls

Eleanor used this coach when she went to stay with her Weatherly relatives in Berwickshire in June 1804.

Although relatively well-to-do, John Weatherly did not own a gig or carriage; local travel for the family was usually on horseback – or on foot. Eleanor regularly walked distances of up to five miles on roughly made roads, without the benefit of modern day footwear. In one year she bought three pairs of black leather shoes, perhaps an indication of her walking habits rather than a fashion statement.

The long serving postmaster at Belford was William Bugg, who features regularly in the diary, socialising at tea and supper parties. Evidently he was not the most efficient postmaster, reprimanded on occasions for not giving his full attention to the letters – perhaps he was too occupied elsewhere.

Permission had been sought in 1746 to hold a market in the town and later two annual fairs were established. One at Whitsuntide known as the Lamb Fair and another held ahead of Michaelmas, which marked the start of autumn. There are no surviving local details for these events in 1804, but in rural areas there was usually an agricultural element to these gatherings and an opportunity for hiring servants. Traditionally the fairs were linked to a saint or feast day and as crowd pleasers would offer entertainment such as side shows, juggling and competitions. There were also booths selling alcohol and perhaps the likes of gingerbread and pies.

A one mile racecourse was constructed to the south west of the town on Belford moor. According to Whyte's 'History of the British Turf', racing was held here from 1838 until 1868. However, we have an account of racing as early as 1804; a race poster for 1815 survives and the course is clearly marked on Greenwood's map of Northumberland dated 1828.

Either Mr Whyte was mistaken or perhaps the course was not officially recognised. A race week held in September, together with its attendant assemblies and theatre performances, became a popular annual event. The location of the theatre in Belford is not known; only advertising posters and the diary entries alert us to its existence. As the Blue Bell sold theatre tickets it is quite likely that performances were held nearby. Groups of players travelled on regular circuits between market towns and often set up their own theatres, which opened for limited periods.

The extensive building programme initiated by Dixon increased the population and attracted many people from across the Scottish Border. The result made for an interesting mix of religious views. Presbyterian families greatly out-numbered those of the Church of England. In 1776 the first dissenters' meeting house was built, known as the 'Scotch' church. Following a split with the Church of Scotland, the Secession church was formed and almost immediately a dispute arose in Belford regarding the choice of a minister. As a result a second meeting house, known as the Erskine church after its founder, was established in the town.

The small parish church dedicated to St Mary held two services each Sunday. The sacrament of communion was only administered four times a year, on feast days at Easter, Whitsun, Michaelmas and Christmas; a public service was also held on these occasions. There was no place of worship for Catholics. Mostly they sought employment elsewhere, and a handful of itinerant Methodist preachers held services in private houses.

When the younger Abraham Dixon died childless in 1782, he left his estate to his great nephew Arthur George Onslow, then a minor. With an absentee squire, the social void was filled by Sir Carnaby and Lady Haggerston. The estate was managed by Thomas Adams, an Alnwick solicitor, and two Belford based land agents, firstly Henry Barber until his death in 1790 and later John Dinning. On reaching his majority, Onslow decided to sell. However as the combined estates proved too costly for would be purchasers, the estates were split and John Weatherly was able to purchase part of the Easington bundle in 1805. William Clark finally bought the Belford estate in 1810.

Britain was at war with France in 1804, even in Northumberland the threat of an invasion was very real. Volunteer Militias were raised and trained to delay and disrupt the enemy until regular forces could be deployed. The Percy Tenantry was raised by the Duke of Northumberland. The Glendale Cavalry was raised by the 4th Earl of Tankerville whose family seat was at Chillingham Castle; the family also owned land at Ross in Belford parish. The volunteers, including Eleanor's brother James, were required to own a horse and rifle and spend time each year in training with the regular army.

The Royal Greenwich Hospital was a landowner of some note in the local area. The Derwentwater estates, held mainly in Northumberland, were granted to the hospital in 1735 as a means for the charity to support itself. These estates were the confiscated property of the Earl of Derwentwater who was executed following his part in the Jacobite uprising of 1715. In 1794 an advertisement was placed in the London Gazette offering farms and estates for let in Northumberland – among which were Scremerston, Spindleston, Outchester, Glororum and Chester Hill. It seems the charity Commissioners inspected these properties from time to time; Eleanor records such a visit in 1805.

Under Dixon's influence, a small harbour at Budle was constructed for the export of grain from the corn mills at Waren and Spindleston. Further down the coast, Bamburgh castle having been rescued from ruin by Nathaniel Crewe, Bishop of Durham following his marriage to Dorothy Forster in 1700, was under the care of his charitable trust. Within the castle the trustees of Lord Crewe's charity administered schools for girls and boys, a dispensary, and kept watch for shipwrecks.

Berwick upon Tweed, no stranger to frequent incursions across the Scottish border, became one of the first places in the country to boast a purpose built barracks and was a bustling garrison town in 1804. Also a busy trading port, enterprising ship builders developed the fast sailing 'Berwick Smack', so important for exports, particularly the salmon trade for which the Tweed was famed. At a cost of one and a half guineas, passengers such as Nicholas Weatherly could also avail themselves of these frequent fast sailings to London.

Still in evidence today, the Kings Arms on Hide Hill was a stopping place for both the Mail and Union coaches. The theatre just behind the inn was converted from a former distillery around 1798, and reportedly fitted out by Mr Kemble, an actor manager. The Kembles were a family of actors who reigned over the British stage for decades; numbered amongst them was the renowned actress, Mrs Sarah Siddons. Audiences in these Georgian theatres were by no means as well behaved as their modern day counterparts; often noisy and unruly as they chatted and vied for better seats during performances. The theatre with its flimsy scenery, wooden interiors and somewhat dangerous lighting, was always a fire risk.

The race course at Lamberton lay in Berwickshire some four miles north of Berwick. Racing started in 1785 and continued as an annual summer event until 1837 – the race week ball was a highlight of the Berwick social calendar. The Lamberton meeting was obviously an event of some importance; local newspapers report attendances upwards of 2000 and confirm that it boasted a grandstand. On July 4th in 1804, the stairs of the grandstand collapsed causing many serious injuries. Eleanor attended on that day, but curiously makes no mention of the incident in her diary.

BELFORD
Festival Races.

TO BE RUN FOR
On *MONDAY, 25th of September*, 1815,

AN ELEGANT

SILVER TANKARD,

By any Horse, Mare, or Gelding, that never started for Fifty Pounds, or won above the value of Thirty Pounds, at any one time, (matches excepted); to carry 8 Stone—Three Miles Heats—Three Horses to start, or no Race.

The Same Day,

A HANDSOME SADDLE,

By any Horse, &c. that never won above the value of Ten Pounds.—Two Miles Heats—Catch Weight.

ALSO,

A FASHIONABLE BRIDLE,

By Ponies not exceeding Thirteen Hands high—One Mile Heats—Catch Weight,

The Horses to be entered between the Hours of 11 and 12 o'clock on the day of Running, at Mr Scrowther's, Black-Swan Inn.

Entrance for the Tankard 5s.—for the Saddle, 2s. 6d and for the Bridle 1s.—Entrance at the Post to pay Double.

To Start precisely at 2 o'clock.

MR TAYLOR,
MR BURN,
MR SCROWTHER, } STEWARDS.
MR S. ROGERS,
MR M'DONALD,

MATTHEW ROBERTSON, Clerk of the Course.

Should any dispute arise, to be settled by the Stewards.

The Winner of the Cup to pay 5s. towards further diversion.

Stewards for the ensuing Year will be appointed upon the Race-Ground.

N. B. The Theatre will be open during the Race Week.

ASSEMBLIES AS USUAL.

Davison, Printer, Alnwick.

5: A poster for the 1815 horse races at Belford

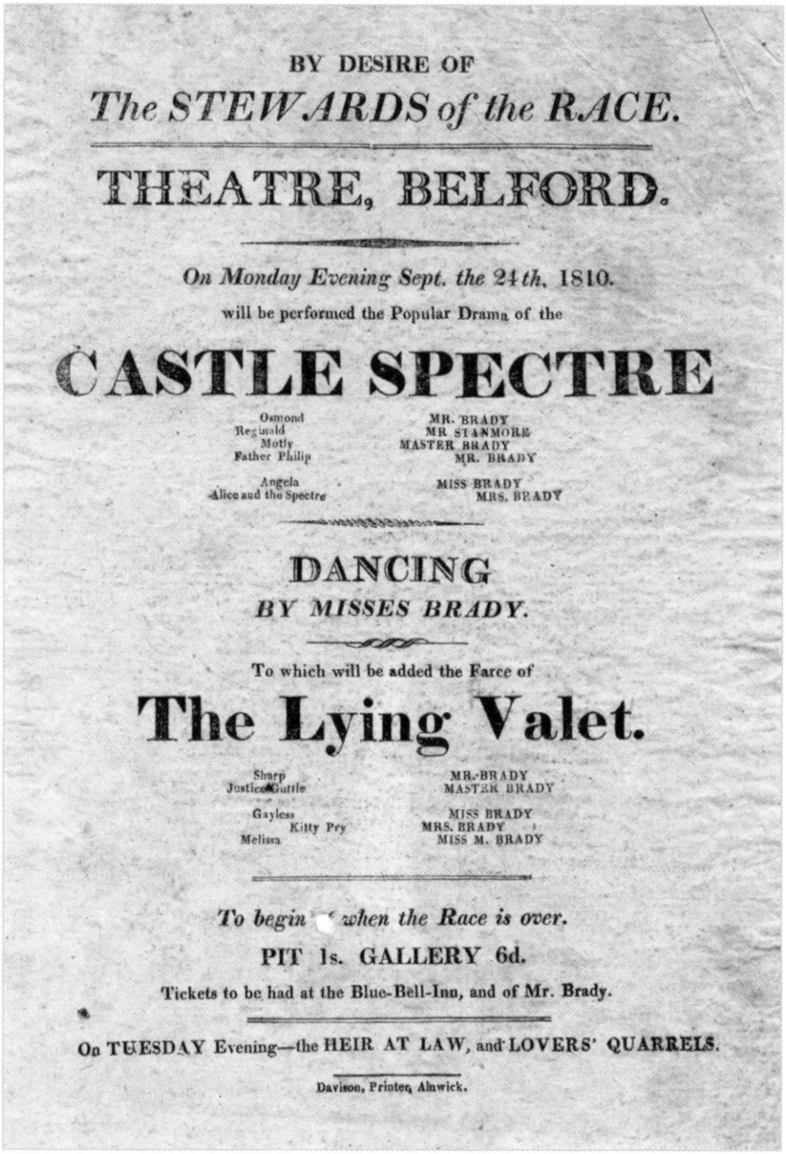

BY DESIRE OF

The STEWARDS of the RACE.

THEATRE, BELFORD.

On Monday Evening Sept. the 24th, 1810.

will be performed the Popular Drama of the

CASTLE SPECTRE

Osmond	MR. BRADY
Reginald	MR STANMORE
Motly	MASTER BRADY
Father Philip	MR. BRADY
Angela	MISS BRADY
Alice and the Spectre	MRS. BRADY

DANCING

BY MISSES BRADY.

To which will be added the Farce of

The Lying Valet.

Sharp	MR. BRADY
Justice Guttle	MASTER BRADY
Gayless	MISS BRADY
Kitty Pry	MRS. BRADY
Melissa	MISS M. BRADY

To begin ' when the Race is over.

PIT 1s. GALLERY 6d.

Tickets to be had at the Blue-Bell-Inn, and of Mr. Brady.

On TUESDAY Evening—the HEIR AT LAW, and LOVERS' QUARRELS.

Davison, Printer, Alnwick.

6: A poster for the theatre in Belford in 1810

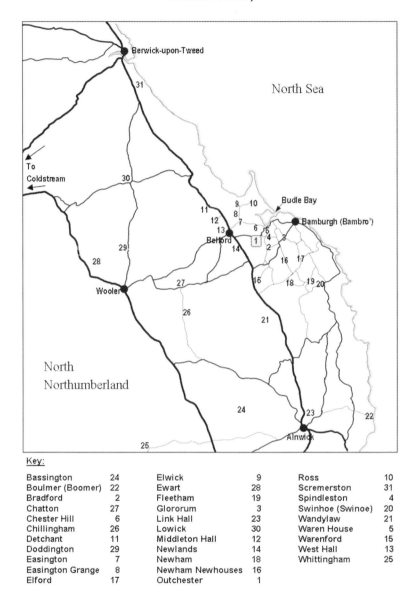

Key:

Bassington	24	Elwick	9	Ross	10
Boulmer (Boomer)	22	Ewart	28	Scremerston	31
Bradford	2	Fleetham	19	Spindleston	4
Chatton	27	Glororum	3	Swinhoe (Swinoe)	20
Chester Hill	6	Link Hall	23	Wandylaw	21
Chillingham	26	Lowick	30	Waren House	5
Detchant	11	Middleton Hall	12	Warenford	15
Doddington	29	Newlands	14	West Hall	13
Easington	7	Newham	18	Whittingham	25
Easington Grange	8	Newham Newhouses	16		
Elford	17	Outchester	1		

7: A map of the Belford area, showing places mentioned in the diary

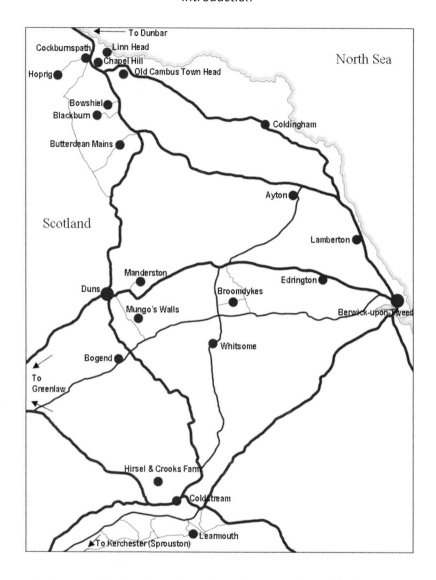

8: A map of the Borders, showing places mentioned in the diary

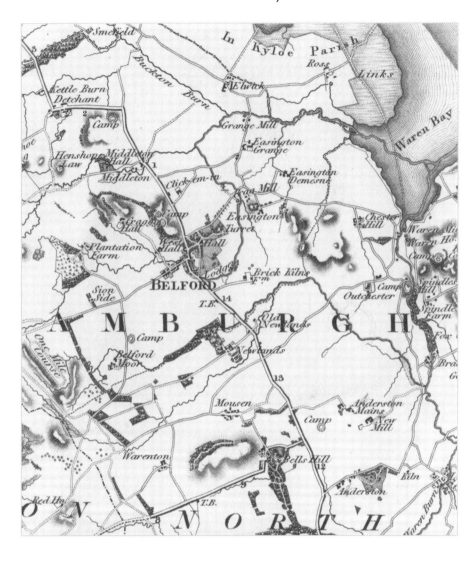

9: An extract from Greenwood's map of 1828, showing the race course to the south-west of Belford

Eleanor's Diary - 1804

Preface

Should curiosity induce
any person to read this book I hope they
will excuse repititions

Eleanor Weatherly
Culchester
1806

14

January

Sunday 1st

Read a sermon on the improvement of time, being appropriate for this day. James wrote to Lieutenant Younghusband – the letter was addressed to him at Carlisle, I wrote the postscript. My cousin W. Weatherly of Dunbar dined here and stopped all night - a fine day.

Monday 2nd

My Father and brothers dined at Bradford. Mrs Hall and apprentice were here making our lace muslin gowns for the Belford dance – Miss Margaret Younghusband sent me a rye loaf for a New Year's gift – mended my white shoes - a remarkable good day.

Tuesday 3rd

Was up at 7 o'clock – had a charming walk – wrote a letter to Miss Dinning before breakfast – made a pair of shoe bows – went to Newlands to tea, from there to the Belford ball - had a ticket from John Younghusband. I danced the first two dances with Ensign Barber – two with John Younghusband and four with William Mole – the last two with Harry Dinning. The ball broke up at two o'clock, we returned to Newlands, and at supper had an extra glass of wine to the health of Cornet George Younghusband, this being his Birth Day – the weather frosty.

Wednesday 4th

Was in the breakfast parlour at half past 8 o'clock, had a tête a tête with Mr H Dinning until nine when Miss Sanderson, Miss D and Susan made their debut. After breakfast, Miss Bab Dinning, Miss Sanderson, Susan and myself took a walk to Belford West Hall, escorted by Captain Sanderson senior and the Reverend Mr Dawson. Sarah Redpeth did not look well this morning, but Miss Bawtree looked interestingly lovely. We came back to Newlands to dinner with an addition to the party, Mr Sandy Thompson of Scremerston and his sister Betsy, with Mr Trotter of Middleton.

Messrs Sanderson and Miss Sanderson went home after dinner, the rest of the company stopped to tea. Mr William Mole and my father came to Newlands in the afternoon and we had a charming dance after tea – Mr Dawson is a very lame dancer. Miss Dinning did not dance with as much spirit as she used to do, having lost her heart the night before at the ball. Miss B.D. sported some new steps which I vainly tried to imitate, but did not succeed. We came home before nine o'clock – William Mole would have accompanied us to Outchester, had not my Father wished him goodnight at the road that takes off to Chesterhill. I was so vexed that I went to bed without my supper – weather still frosty.

Thursday 5th

Rather fatigued – read most part of the day as I could not settle to work – won 8 pence at cards – the weather very stormy, had some heavy showers of hail and snow.

Friday 6th

Mr Antony Barber drank tea here – he had on a fashionable drab greatcoat – Mr Walton was also here and lost 11 pence at cards – Mr A.B and I were partners, we won fourteen pence – weather still continues stormy

Saturday 7th

Susan and I had a quarrel today because she would not give me a piece of clout[1] to mend my morning gown, we exchanged a few blows and I came off victorious – had a long letter from Miss B. Dinning enclosing the fashions for the year 1804 – one of our servants drawn for the Militia won 3d – a hard frost and showers of snow.

Sunday 8th

There has been a very great fall of snow last night – the roads are all blocked up – I cannot get to Warenford – had a fire on in our room – Nichol had his usual search for his catechism, but could not find it – nor never can.

Monday 9th

Mr Taylor of Fleetham called here this morning – had a card from West Hall inviting us to dine there on Thursday, won a shilling at cards – this day has been very stormy, a great deal of rain and sleet.

Tuesday 10th

This day has been replete with disappointments and hopes. My Father says we are not to go to West Hall on Thursday – I lost my dinner with the hare pudding being too salt – lost 1/6 at cards and last of all lost my temper – rainy day

---

[1] Piece of cloth for patching

Wednesday 11th

Wrote a letter to Miss B Dinning – had a letter from Miss Younghusband with a horse for me to come to Elwick – I did not go but sent Susan - had also a letter from Miss Dinning – a fine frosty day.

Thursday 12th

Had a letter from Miss Margaret Younghusband, I had not time to answer it – we went to West Hall to dinner and spent the evening – where we had a pleasant dance. Gents were very civil - a showery day.

Friday 13th

James had a letter from Lieutenant Younghusband, Carlisle – I have been very busy this morning pickling cabbage – had a letter from Miss Bawtree. Susan came home from Elwick, had a great packet of news – a pleasant day.

Saturday 14th

Had a letter from R.Y.[2] Mr Watson called this morning – Mr Noble and Mr Harry Barber called but did not stop to tea, as I was at Newham Newhouses, Wrote an answer to R.Y's letter – won a shilling at cards – got a very severe cold – a fresh weather day.

Sunday 15th

Learned a psalm and 6 verses of a chapter[3] – had a letter from my cousin of Bowshiel, and a parcel from Edinbro' – James went to Haddington – a very rainy day.

Monday 16th

Mr Gay and Mr Sanderson of Swinoe[4] called – we had a roast pig to dinner – Miss Dinnings were here to tea – James came home from the Drill very ill, has got a severe cold – have such trouble in my eyes I can hardly see to write – weather still continues rainy.

Tuesday 17th

I won a shilling from Susan about the sun rising – was dressed rather comical today, had on a buff gown – green checked handkerchief – purple

---

[2] Robert Younghusband
[3] Possibly an alternative to church attendance
[4] Swinhoe

stock – black velvet round my head – with a large green shade – had to go to bed after tea was so ill – fine fresh day.

Wednesday 18th

Had a letter from Miss Dinning for Susan and I to go to Newlands, but cannot get a horse for Nick is riding my Father's black Galloway – rainy day.

Thursday 19th

Had a present of a turkey from Miss Young – a letter from Miss Dinning – saw four smart beaux but could not prevail upon one of them to stop to tea – lost a shilling at cards – fine day.

Friday 20th

Mr Barber of Doddington dined here – had Chatto Watson to tea – wrote a letter to Miss Dinning – lost 6d at cards – a showery day.

Saturday 21st

Mr William Mole and Mr William Watson called – after them Mr Joseph Watson and Jonney. Mr Yellowly spent the afternoon with us, had a letter from Miss Dinning – two from Miss Watson and one from Lieutenant Younghusband with a handsome present. Played at cards, neither lost nor won – answered all the letters I received – a pleasant day, had some showers of rain.

Sunday 22nd

Breakfast at Newlands – went to Belford church – from there to Wandylaw with Miss Dinnings and Harry. Mr Richardson came here at 10 o'clock and spent the day with my Father – rain in the morning – after that a pleasant day.

Monday 23rd

Wrote to Mr Watson. Mr Yellowly and John and Chatto Watson called – Mr Rogers drank tea with us – a pleasant day.

Tuesday 24th

Made all the button holes of Edward Hall's shirts – weather still continues fresh.

Wednesday 25th

There has been a great fall of rain last night – the waters are all up – not one in this neighbourhood is fordable. Mr Yellowly called – Susan and I had a dispute about making the tea – neither of us would do it – so my Father did it himself – lost 1/6 at cards.

Thursday 26th

My Father was from home. The Miss Dinnings came down in the afternoon- we were just comfortably sat around the fireside when a servant came for them to go home, as Mr & Mrs Trotter and Mr & Mrs Patterson had come to Newlands to tea. I wrote to the milliner – rained in the morning but pleasant evening.

Friday 27th

I wrote a letter for one of the servants to her husband – went to Newlands to tea – arrived there before they sat down to dinner. Barbara, Harry and I took a ride to Belford – Harry treat us with sweetmeats – had a rubber at cards – weather the same as yesterday.

Saturday 28th

Had a letter from Lieutenant Younghusband – a very rainy day.

Sunday 29th

Learned 6 verses of a Chapter – drank tea at Spindleston – a remarkable fine day.

Monday 30th

Was up at 7 o'clock – John Watson, William and Richard Wood called – we had Mr Ostens to tea – I won a shilling from him with betting at cards – a very rainy day.

Tuesday 31st

Had a letter from Miss Dinning and answered it – Mr Young was here today packing wool. James, Susan and I went to Newlands to tea where we met Mr Bugg, Miss Margaret Younghusband and John and Miss Jonstone of Bywell. We had a dance and several songs from Mr Bugg and Miss Dinning, we stayed to supper – a very fine day.

February

Wednesday 1ˢᵗ

Quite alone – a very fine day.

Thursday 2ⁿᵈ

We were all very much alarmed this morning by a report that the French are landed in Scotland. The Glendale Cavalry[5] are gone to Alnwick to join the Percy Tenantry. J. Younghusband called on James and William Watson - we had a visit from Mr McQueen, a call from Mr Walton and Chatto Watson in the evening had a letter from Miss Dinning – a very fine day but rain in the evening – lost 1/6 at cards but got it again.

Friday 3ʳᵈ

The report was false – the Beacons were lighted by seeing some whins on fire – James came home from Alnwick this afternoon very much mortified that he had not seen some of the French dogs. Miss B Dinning came here in the morning and spent the day with us – her sister came after dinner. We took a walk to Spindleston. I won seventeen pence at cards – we amused ourselves tonight by blacking each other's faces. This day has been very pleasant but towards evening remarkably stormy.

Saturday 4ᵗʰ

Miss Dinnings stayed here last night – we did not go to bed until 1 o'clock this morning talking about a dance my Father promises to give us. I was awakened out of my sleep by a young man rapping at the door just as I was finishing a pleasant dream. James wrote a card to Mr Fenwick Compton enclosing a ticket to him for the Belford dance. I have been very busy today making marmalade – won two pence at cards. I have bet a shilling with James about Miss Jonstone's aromatic vinegar box – stormy day, hail and sleet.

Sunday 5ᵗʰ

Was at Warenford Meeting. Mr Anthony Barber, Belford and Mr William Barber, Boomer[6] came here to tea. The frost has been very intense last night.

Monday 6ᵗʰ

---

[5] Volunteer militia
[6] Boulmer

Wrote to Miss Dinning – had an answer – the weather still continues frosty.

Tuesday 7th

Went to Newlands to tea from there to Mr Calvert's second subscription ball – danced with Mr Harry Dinning, Mr William Barber, Mr William Mole, Mr William Walton and Mr Edward George. We were honoured by the presence of Sir Carnaby and Lady Haggerston, Sir Thomas Stanley and Miss Haggerston – the room was crowded as there were near a hundred people in it – broke up at 4 o'clock. Weather frosty yet.

Wednesday 8th

Mr Scott, Mr Sandy Thompson of Scremerston, Captain Humble. Lieutenant Sanderson breakfasted here. We saw a fox chase from the window and likewise saw Mr Harry Dinning take the brush – he presented to me – Mr Bugg came to tea, and my brother James. We left Newlands soon after tea and lost the road in coming home - fresh weather.

Thursday 9th

Wrote to Miss Dinning – had two letters from Miss B.D. – a very pleasant morning but rainy afternoon.

Friday 10th

Miss Younghusband and Miss Werges of Horton drank tea here – Miss Y stopped all night as it was so dark she durst not drive the gig, so James had to be charioteer to Miss Werges – won two shillings at cards. Weather the same as yesterday.

Saturday 11th

Richard Wood came for Margaret before we sat down to breakfast. Harry Dinning drank tea here, he came to take leave of us before he went to Edinbro' and was very civil. Been in remarkably low spirits today – won eleven pence at Lieu[7] – the weather still continues stormy.

Sunday 12th

Had a card from Mr Richardson this morning before I was out of 'mon lit' – answered Mr R's card. We were at Belford church today – sat in Younghusband's seat. Mr Cook treat us with Ratafie – took very ill after I came home and had to go to bed. Read 3 sermons – weather frosty.

---

[7] Loo – game played with three or five cards

Monday 13th

Wrote a card to Miss Watson and one to Miss Younghusband – had an answer from Mis Y-h-d. Called at Newlands on my road to Belford – bought a tea kettle – came to Newlands to tea – rode home behind James on his mare, the first time she ever carried double - fine frosty day.

Tuesday 14th

Wrote a note to Miss Dinning had an answer from her and one from Bab – won two pence at cards. Weather still continues frosty.

Wednesday 15th

Made an Italian cheese – wrote to Miss Dinning had an answer – been in very low spirits today – cold frost, winds and showers of rain.

Thursday 16th

Had a large party to tea and supper and a dance. The Younghusbands, Woods, Dinnings, Watsons and Moles. We danced till 4 o'clock – Miss Walton and Miss Bawtrie went home immediately after supper. Miss Y-h-d and Miss Dinnings stayed all night. James was very civil to the ladies – fresh weather.

Friday 17th

Mr William Mole called this morning with my sash. Miss Dinnings went home to dinner – we had a charming walk by the fields, but rather dirty – won 6 pence at cards.

Saturday 18th

Susan and I were at wars this morning – I beat her until she wept – Miss Margaret Younghusband left us about 12 o'clock, her cousin Wood called for her. I have had a very busy day cleaning the closets – have been contriving a dress to have on at Elwick next week – as I hear we are to have a dance – could not get a game at cards tonight as I was short of cash – uncommon fine day.

Sunday 19th

Susan, Nichol and I were at Newham Newhouses to tea, James was at Waren to tea – had a call from Mr Steven Rogers and Mr Charles Macdonald – a fine day.

Monday 20ᵗʰ

Had a letter from Lieutenant Younghusband, wrote to Miss Watson and Miss B Dinning – had an answer and an invitation to Newlands to tea this afternoon this being Mr Harry's Birth Day. We were there rather early – spent a very pleasant afternoon – had a game at Commerce[8] and won the pool which was 13/6 – stayed to supper. Weather is still good.

Tuesday 21ˢᵗ

Miss Charlotte Macdonald and her brother Charles called – Mr Ross came here to dinner – Susan and James are gone to Bassington – fine day, rather frosty.

Wednesday 22ⁿᵈ

When we were all setting off for our beds last night. Mr Anthony Barber and Mr Archbold of Berwick came to supper – they stayed until a very late hour. Mr Walton and Charles Macdonald drank tea here – we had a game at cards – I lost sixpence – a remarkable fine day.

Thursday 23ʳᵈ

Quite alone – won seven pence at cards – a hazy day, some showers of hail.

Friday 24ᵗʰ

Took pottage to my breakfast – Mr William Walton called – won sixpence at cards. This day has been remarkably cold and stormy.

Saturday 25ᵗʰ

James and I took a ride to Belford after dinner – we afterwards went to Elwick – Mr Edward Gray was also there. Played at cards – I had John Y[9] for a partner – won a shilling – very stormy day.

Sunday 26ᵗʰ

I forgot to mention that Mr Trotter of Kerchesters called yesterday morning. Indeed this morning I did not know what I was about, for I sugared all the tea cups twice – but I always commit a multiplicity of mistakes after seeing John Y. James and I took a ride out this morning we called at Glororum came round by Bambro' next to Budle Telegraph – then made the best of our way home – a remarkable pleasant day, but rather cold.

---

[8] Trading card game
[9] John Younghusband

Monday 27th

I expected to have gone today to see Lord Ossoulton's[10] Corps inspected – but alas I am disappointed. Mr Yellowly called after dinner – Miss Dinning and Miss Wilson of Alnwick came and drank tea with us – we had a game at Lieu – I was in partnership with Barbara – we won ten pence – weather rather stormy.

Tuesday 28th

My cousin William Weatherly of Dunbar came here to tea – we had a game at Lieu. Susan and I went halfs – we lost 1/6 – cold day.

Wednesday 29th

Had a pig merchant here this morning – he and I could not agree about the price so did no business. Spun a clip of yarn before 4 o'clock – Miss Bawtree and Miss Watson were out walking – they saw me and called for me to go to Waren with them. I went and spent the evening – played at cards – won six pence – pleasant frosty day. My Father and cousin with James and Susan all went to Newham Newhouses to dinner – Susan has lost all her money and came home in a very sore temper. I have been very busy reeling my yarn tonight.

---

[10] Captain of the Glendale Cavalry, son of the Earl of Tankerville

March

Thursday 1st

Susan, James and I went up to Newlands this afternoon – had a dance to a fiddle, clarinet, triangle, pianoforte – saw Miss Dinnings and Miss Wilson's dress for the Belford ball. Frost some showers of snow. Miss Wilson and Captain Burns were at Newlands.

Friday 2nd

Mr John Younghusband spent the day with us – wrote to Miss B Dinning – had an answer- got a ticket for the ball from Mr Walton and one from Mr Joseph Mole – will give Mr Waltons to Susan - won sixpence at Whist and three pence at Watch the Ten[11] – snow on the ground, frosty.

Saturday 3rd

Had Mr Walton to tea and we drank tea by daylight and had a hand at cards before the candle was brought in – I lost nine pence – some showers of snow – frosty.

Sunday 4th

Wrote a letter last night to Miss Tait which I omitted to write down – was at Warenford Meeting today – very stormy.

Monday 5th

I have been six times dressed in my ball gown which I'm to have on tomorrow night – won a shilling at cards – this day has been very stormy, showers of sleet.

Tuesday 6th

Mr Young and Mr Trotter with my cousin William Weatherly dined here. Susan and I dressed to go to the ball at Belford, I was the last that came into the room – danced the first two dances with Mr Thomas Smith – next with Mr Archbold then with Cornet Grieve Smith – and last with Mr Donaldson. Mr Pringle very civil to Miss Wilson – ball broke up at 5 o'clock – went home with the Newlands party – rainy day.

---

[11] Game where ten is the most valuable card

Wednesday 7th

Newlands – Mr Thompson and Miss Betsy, Miss Atkinson, Miss Wilson, Mr and Miss Sanderson, Mr and Miss Henderson, Susan and self breakfasted here. Most of them went home to dinner, but we as usual spent the day – James came up to tea – came home about 8 o'clock – fine day.

Thursday 8th

Quite alone today – began to spin the coarse Lint – dry day.

Friday 9th

Quite alone – very rainy day.

Saturday 10th

Quite alone – a remarkable fine day

Sunday 11th

Both Susan and I were at Warenford Meeting today - we took a walk to Spindleston – after dinner I began to read through the Testament – fine day.

Monday 12th

Nichol had a letter from Harry Dinning – we were at Newlands to tea this afternoon, where we met Miss Mary Ann Selby – my cousin William Weatherly is here tonight – wrote to Miss Redpeth and my cousin Grace Hood - a very fine day.

Tuesday 13th

Susan and my Father are gone to Scotland – I took a walk to Spindleston to call on Mrs Crisp – Nichol and I went to Mr Forsters of Glororum to tea – a very fine day.

Wednesday 14th

Mr John Younghusband and Mr William Walton called on James at 7 o'clock this morning – wrote to Miss Dinning and had two letters from her – the Miss Ds called here in the afternoon. I went to Elwick with them to tea where we met Mr Joe Mole – I lost sixpence at cards – a remarkable fine day.

Thursday 15th

Miss Dinnings drank tea here – I lost sixpence at cards. This is James's Birth Day – Barbara learned me a new step – rainy day.

Friday 16th

Mr Gray of Swinoe called this morning – Mr Richardson called after dinner – had a letter from Miss Dinning – I went to Newlands to tea – came home at 10 o'clock – rainy day.

Saturday 17th

Quite alone today, we expected Miss Forster and Mr Richardson, but suppose the weather has prevented them as it has rained incessantly this whole day. I have spun a quarter pound of Lint – altered a Habit skirt[12] and hemmed 4 coarse towels today.

Sunday 18th

James and I were at Belford church, went to Newlands to dinner where we met Mr Jobling – the Miss Dinnings came home with me to tea – Mr William Watson was also here to tea – this is Carling Sunday[13] – had a letter from Susan - fine day but some showers of hail.

Monday 19th

The kitchen maid and I spun half a spignol[14] of yarn today – my Father and uncle David came from Scotland – a fine frosty day but rather cold.

Tuesday 20th

My uncle left us this morning – wrote to Miss B Dinning – had a letter from both her and Miss D - cold frosty day – some showers of hail.

Wednesday 21st

Mr Ostens, Mr Scott and Mr Yellowly called after dinner – Mrs Hall drank tea here – I had a walk as far as the turnpike after tea – fine frosty day.

Thursday 22nd

Miss Dinnings were here to tea – cold frosty day.

---

[12] Skirt for riding side saddle

[13] Fifth Sunday in Lent. Originally Care Sunday. It was the custom in North East England to eat dried peas, soaked then fried in butter – known as Carlings

[14] In spinning terms four hanks make a spinnle [spignol], and twelve cuts are a hank or slip. These words are now unknown save to old people. (R.O Heslop, Northumberland words 1892)

Friday 23rd

Mr Barber of Doddington called, Mr John Younghusband called on me to go to Newlands – where we met with Mrs and Miss Goodwill, and William Watson, stopped till supper – a fine frosty day.

Saturday 24th

Mr Watson breakfasted here – James and I drank tea at Spindleston where we met Miss Bawtree and the Waren family – cold day showers of hail and sleet.

Sunday 25th

John Younghusband called but I was at Warenford Meeting so did not see him – Mr Mole of Whittingham sat in our pew today – I met Mr Pratt on our road home – Nichol and I went to Newlands to tea – Miss Dinning had a letter from Susan- stormy day , snow.

Monday 26th

Miss Bawtree, Miss Watson, Chatto Watson and Miss Dinnings were here to tea – lost a shilling at cards – stormy wet day.

Tuesday 27th

James was at Belford today at the decision of some bets that were made at Mr Yellowlys that day - they dined there – cold day.

Wednesday 28th

Miss Dinning called on her way to Swinoe – I took a ride as far as Miss Youngs along with her – wrote to Susan. I was up this morning at 7 o'clock – a remarkable fine day – badly off for pens.

Thursday 29th

William Watson was here to breakfast at 7 o'clock – James and he went to the Drill – Barbara Dinning called after tea – fine day some showers of rain.

Friday 30th

This being Good Friday I went to Belford church – from there to Wandylaw with Miss B. Dinning to dinner – saw a great number of officers at Belford – a remarkable fine day – James was sowing wheat today late.

Saturday 31ˢᵗ

John Younghusband called this morning as did Mr Walton – had John Younghusband to tea – got my ball gown home from Edinburgh, all over silver trimming with velvet sleeves – a stormy day, hail.

April

Sunday 1st

I had a walk with James through the fields, seeing the lambs – fine cold day.

Monday 2nd

Got an April fool letter from Alnwick – been busy today altering my ball dress – Miss Jemima Barber was here to tea – had a walk to Spindleston Hills – fine day.

Tuesday 3rd

Rode up to Newlands at 3 o'clock, had my hair dressed at 4 by Mr Cousins – drank tea at 5 – finished dressing at 7 o'clock – was led into the ball by Mr Dinning – danced the 2 first dances with Lieutenant Sanderson, next with Mr Werges – then with Mr Forster and the last with Mr John Wood Younghusband. Returned to Newlands at half past 3 o'clock, supped and went to bed at 4 o'clock – this is Calvert's last subscription ball – showery day.

Wednesday 4th

Newlands – rose at 10 o'clock quite refreshed- had 4 slices of tongue, 3 of ham, an egg and three cups of tea to my breakfast. At eleven Mr Sandy Thompson, his nephew Mr Harriot, Mr Trotter, James and Nichol came to dinner. At twelve Mr Dawson made his debut – we had a dance after dinner – I had Sandy for a partner. Miss Sanderson went home to tea – Mr Dawson took his departure at the same time – all the beaux went away early – Mr Bugg was announced when we were sitting at tea – he stopped to supper – fine day.

Thursday 5th

Newlands – wrote a postscript to a letter from B. Dinning to Susan – we took a ride in the gig to Mrs Trotter of Middleton Hall – drank tea there – I then went home to Outchester on foot – weather changeable, snow, sleet and rain – pleasant evening.

Friday 6th

Spent a very solitary day, took a walk after tea – met with Mr Pringle of Beadnell – had a long chat with him – had a visit from Mr Bugg – he has bought our young horse – wrote a long letter to Susan – this has been a remarkable fine day.

Saturday 7th

Mr Scott of Easington dined here – had a letter from Miss Ronaldson from Edinburgh answering one I wrote her last summer – I have been busy today packing up a box to send to Susan – have sent her my buff dress – this was a pleasant morning, dull evening.

Sunday 8th

Was at Warenford Meeting – saw Mrs Ross's little daughter for the first time – took very ill after I came home – went to bed after dinner – Miss Dinning wrote a card for me to come up to Newlands – I grew immediately better – went up there to tea where I met Mrs & Miss Wastall and Mr Bugg – had a letter from Susan – cold day.

Monday 9th

Mr Henderson of Newton and his son called while we were at dinner – Mr Trotter of Newham drank tea and supped here – cold day.

Tuesday 10th

Mr Gray of Swinoe and Mr Atchison called. My cousin W. Weatherly and Mr Rankin of Berwick and Miss Dinnings drank tea here – went as far as the turnpike with Miss Ds – I without hat or shawl had to walk home – dirty roads – had on my best morocco shoes – lost 1/6 at cards – a cold day, frost winds.

Wednesday 11th

Mr William Wood called this morning with a couple of pens from Mr Younghusband to me – James had a letter from Mr Harry Dinning – wrote to Miss Dinning and had an answer – Mr Rankin, Mr Anderson of Elford and Miss Anderson of Sunderland House drank tea with us – Mr Pattison of Wooler called – James has been at home this whole day – cold frost, winds – finished spinning the coarse Lint begun April 8th.

Thursday 12th

Took a walk to Newlands after dinner – arrived there at 4 o'clock – Bab Dinning and I went to Belford – came to Outchester to tea, had Mr Walton – I walked all the way up to Newlands with Barbara again and got home 5 minutes before nine – cloudy morning – afterwards a pleasant day.

Friday 13th

I expected to have gone to Newlands today but was disappointed as my Father would not allow me to go, I had been so lately there – my cousin William Weatherly came over from Newham Newhouses – had a serious conversation with him about Susan's beaux – he went away after tea – we had a game at cards – I won sixpence – chilly day.

Saturday 14th

Took a walk to Waren this morning – saw Miss Handyside and Mr George Mole – wrote to Susan – I went to Newlands after dinner – Bab met me at the Burn – Mr Harry Dinning of Newcastle and Mr Bugg were there – Miss Dinnings escorted me half way home – Mr George Carnforth came from Alnwick with my Father and James. I did not go to bed until about 1 o'clock – I was sore with laughing at Mr C's droll stories – dull rainy evening.

Sunday 15th

I was at Warenford Meeting – James and Nichol dined at Spindleston with Mr Richardson who had a large party – cold day.

Monday 16th

Mr Carnforth went away after breakfast. William Weatherly came here to dinner – had a letter from Susan and one from each of the Miss Dinnings – wrote to Miss Ronaldson and Miss Hamilton – went to Waren House to tea, afterwards I went in the carriage with Mrs & Miss Watson and Miss Bawtree to Belford to the Silver Miners' concert – the House was crowded – the weather still continues cold.

Tuesday 17th

Miss Dinning and John Younghusband drank tea here – we went home to Newlands with Miss D – pleasant morning but cold evening.

Wednesday 18th

Mr Ostens called – cold day.

Thursday 19th

Mr John Younghusband called – I was at Newlands to tea – wrote to Lieutenant Younghusband – a remarkable stormy day, snow and sleet.

Friday 20th

I went to Newlands after dinner and from there with Miss Dinning to Middleton Hall where we met Mrs Patterson, Miss Romney, Mr Cook, Captain Cook, the Miss Selbys of Detchant and Mr Sandy Thompson – our James and John Younghusband called after tea – we played at Commerce, I won eighteen pence - won a guinea by a bet from a gentleman, but let him off for sixpence – weather exceedingly stormy.

Saturday 21st

Took a walk to Spindleston to see Mr Walton but he was from home – I sat a little while with Mrs Crisp – I have been very busy today amongst my clothes – had a general review – am in rather low spirits – the weather is still very cold – showers of hail this morning.

Sunday 22nd

Was at Mr Thompson's Meeting[15] – William Weatherly dined here – I had a walk this afternoon with Miss Watson, Miss Bawtree and the three little Watsons on Spindleston Hills – pleasant day but frosty.

Monday 23rd

Mr Dinning called while we were sitting at dinner – had John and Yellowly Watson to tea – Miss Forster of Glororum called in the evening – I took a walk as far as Spindleston along with her. The weather seemed quite calm this morning till about noon, snow and sleet afterwards, cold.

Tuesday 24th

Had a letter from Miss B. Dinning, one from Miss Ronaldson and one from my cousin William – wrote to Susan – went up to Newlands to tea – was home before sunset – spun nine cutts of yarn – read a novel – William Weatherly came to supper – I did not get to bed until half after 12 o'clock. The weather is still very wet, had several showers today.

Wednesday 25th

We breakfasted this morning at seven o'clock – William Weatherly went away immediately after – I ate a shoulder of lamb to dinner – Mr Walton called after tea – we had a rubber at Whist – I lost a penny – a very disagreeable wet day.

---

[15] The Erskine Church

Thursday 26th

Was at my wheel this morning before seven o'clock – had John Younghusband and William Walton to breakfast – fresh fine day.

Friday 27th

Was quite alone today until William Humble came at 8 o'clock – he stopped to supper – I got a chest of drawers – had several showers today.

Saturday 28th

Been remarkably busy cleaning out my room – I have got a severe headache with working so hard – I have been very dull all this week, having seen the Miss Dinnings so seldom – the weather is beginning to settle, this has been a very fine day.

Sunday 29th

Was at Warenford Meeting – had a letter from Susan – Miss Dinnings, Mr Bugg and John Younghusband drank tea here – fine day.

Monday 30th

Took a walk to Spindleston after tea – met Miss Watson there, went down to Waren with her – saw Mr Watson and Joe Mole – pleasant day.

May

Tuesday 1ˢᵗ

Had a letter from Miss Watson – a remarkable fine day.

Wednesday 2ⁿᵈ

Wrote to Susan – had a letter from Miss Barbara Dinning – went up to Newlands to tea, where I met Miss Betsy Thompson, Mr & Mrs Trotter and little Matthew and Miss Margaret Trotter. Bab and I took a walk to Belford after tea – it was 10 o'clock before I reached home – fine day.

Thursday 3ʳᵈ

Was up this morning at six o'clock to spin – I spun until seven in the evening and had two slips of yarn – Mr Black came here after tea – thick foggy day, towards evening very rainy.

Friday 4ᵗʰ

Had a letter from Miss Dinning – I went to Newlands this afternoon to angle – Miss Bawtree and Mr & Mrs Wastall were there – we had a charming sail in the boat – Miss Bawtree and I rowed – Mr Joseph Jobson was at Outchester to tea – fine day.

Saturday 5ᵗʰ

Heard of Mrs Ross's death which has put me in low spirits – had a letter from Mr Robert Younghusband, Dublin – I drank tea with Nelly Ray – Mr Walton was here to tea – my cousin John Weatherly of Butterdean Mains came here to spend a few days. I have been uncommonly restless today – I first began to red up[16] my drawers – next to spin – then read – about an hour after that I began to make a watch chain, but I did not finish a job today – at last I found some amusement in the world – a book wrote by Fitz Adam – foggy day.

Sunday 6ᵗʰ

Was at Belford church – Miss Betsy Thompson and Mr Sandy Thompson were in Mr Dinning's pew – I called at Newlands in the morning – went to Newham Newhouses after dinner and called at Bambro' Friars – saw Miss Humble and William – cloudy morning, afterwards pleasant.

---

[16] Tidy up

Monday 7th

Miss Goodwill called to take leave of us before they left Belford – I took a walk as far as Newlands along with her – had a letter from Miss Watson – wrote to B. Dinning, carried the letter myself – was at Spindleston this afternoon – fine day.

Tuesday 8th

I went to Spindleston to breakfast – from there to Bambro' Church to Betty Wilson's wedding – came back to Spindleston to dinner – there was a large party – eight and twenty dined – Miss Dinnings and John Younghusband and Mr Richardson came back to Outchester for supper – we were all very merry when my Father and James made their debut – they were at Link Hall sale – this has been a remarkable fine day.

Wednesday 9th

Wrote to Miss Redpeth – my cousin and Nichol are gone to Scotland – Mr William Humble breakfasted here – Mr Young came to dinner – Miss Humble and her brother came to tea – I was in uncommon low sprits today – weather good.

Thursday 10th

Wrote to Robert Younghusband – fine day.

Friday 11th

Was quite alone today – my Father and James are at Mr Wastall's neep[17] – I dined at 3 o'clock on radishes – Mr Anthony Barber called in the evening – very drunk – fine day but rather cold.

Saturday 12th

Went up to Newlands after dinner – Barbara and I took a walk to Belford – on our way home we met Mr Cook and Mr George Selby – saw Joe Mole – William Humble overtook me at the burn and escorted me to Outchester – Mr Walton and my Father were sitting tête a tête when we arrived – been busy baking rye bread today – fine day.

Sunday 13th

Was at Warenford Meeting – met Mr Pratt – fine day but rather cold.

---

[17] Turnip sale

Monday 14th

James and I went to Newham Newhouses at 10 o'clock – we dined at half past ten – from there we went to Link Hall, Miss Young accompanied us – we drank tea with Mrs Trotter and Miss Richardson – came back to Newhouses to supper – got home about eight o'clock – wrote to the Iron Monger and Cabinet Maker – weather the same as yesterday.

Tuesday 15th

Mr & Mrs Trotter called this morning – Mrs Weatherly and her family came from Dunbar today – Susan returned along with them – I was at Belford Fair but did not stop ten minutes – showery day.

Wednesday 16th

Mrs Weatherly, the children, Marion and I went to Newham Newhouses to dinner – Miss Young, John and I went to Link Hall to put the house in order. Miss Y. went home but I had to stop all night. My cousin David Weatherly was at Outchester – heavy showers this morning, afterwards pleasant.

Thursday 17th

Link Hall – a gentleman called this morning – I don't know his name – he was enquiring after Mr Wilson's family. Mr Young, my brother James and our cousin David came here after dinner – Miss Young was along with them. Mr Scott called after tea – our company all went away at nine o'clock and I was again left in the house with only my cousin William and little John – Miss Younghusband, John and Miss Wood and Miss Dinnings were at Outchester – weather continues much the same.

Friday 18th

My cousin has a sprained arm so I had to be his amanuensis – wrote to Mr Hood. I have been very busy today cooking the dinner for my Father and cousins – my cousin David went home this afternoon. Mrs Weatherly came with the rest of her family about five o'clock which gave me some relief – a dull queer day.

Saturday 19th

Link Hall – Mr Young came here to dinner – Nichol came for me to go home – I stopped to tea, took a walk after and met Captain Wallace – we took our departure at seven o'clock – fine day.

Sunday 20th

All the family are at the Meeting today but myself – Mr Richardson called just as they rode from the door – he and I had a long tête a tête – he stopped until half after one – a pleasant day.

Monday 21st

I forgot to mention last week that I had a letter from Miss Redpeth and one each from my cousin Grace Hood and Miss Wilson, Dunbar. Went up to Newlands, took a walk after tea to Belford and then to West Hall to see Miss Bawtree – a very disagreeable day.

Tuesday 22nd

Susan went to Whitsunbank[18] with Miss B Dinning and Miss Bawtree – I went up to Newlands with Miss Dinning who called on me this morning – we spent a very pleasant day – had a sail in the boat after tea. The company all came from the Fair about nine o'clock – Mr Humble, Cook, Younghusband, Chatto Watson, little Patterson, and my brother escorted the ladies home – I rode behind J. Younghusband to Outchester – Humble also came home with me – a fine day.

Wednesday 23rd

Was up twice to the turnpike to meet Susan – Dr Patterson and Mr Pratt passed me on the road – showery day.

Thursday 24th

I drank tea this afternoon at West Hall with Miss Bawtree and Mrs Humble – called at Mrs Barbers – met with a beau at West Hall, very civil – a disagreeable day – rain.

Friday 25th

This is a general Feast[19] – I was at Belford church – John Younghusband came here after dinner and my cousin from Link Hall. Miss Watson came up for us to go to a wedding that was at Spindleston Mill – we all went down and drank tea with the bride – met with a great deal of civility – we came back to Outchester with the addition of Mr Richardson and the Watsons – we escorted Miss Watson to Waren House – saw Miss Bawtree there.

---

[18] Fair held every Whit Tuesday on a site five miles to the south-east of Wooler
[19] Religious festival

Saturday 26th

Susan and I took a walk to Spindleston – I called on Mr Walton – fine day.

Sunday 27th

I was at Warenford Meeting – William Weatherly was here to dinner – we were at Newlands to tea – fine day but rather dull.

Monday 28th

Mr Trotter of Newham, Mr Dinning and his brother called this morning – Miss Bab Dinning came down this afternoon – we took a walk to Belford after tea – a fine day, shower of rain.

Tuesday 29th

Had a letter from Miss B Dinning – Mr Walton and Mr Barber of Doddington called – Mr B. was civil – a disagreeable cold day.

Wednesday 30th

Quite alone – a fine day.

Thursday 31st

Susan, James and I took our breakfast with Mrs Davidson – made a sleeping gown – had a baking – bottled a cask of rum. This day has been uncommonly windy, so much so, that when I was out getting a walk, the wind blew me over – I was obliged to get hold of a plough stilt[20] – a shower of rain towards evening.

---

[20] Handle

June

Friday 1st

Mr Dinning and his brother and Mr Yellowly dined here – we had chicken and gooseberries to dinner for the first time this season – Mr Richardson came in the morning and spent the day – fine day.

Saturday 2nd

Miss Dinnings came down after tea to get some money from my Father to buy us hats in Newcastle – had a deal to do before he would part with the ready – James is very ill tonight of a sore throat – fine day.

Sunday 3rd

Had a letter from Lieutenant Younghusband, Ireland – my cousins from Link Hall came from Warenford Meeting here to dinner. Mrs Weatherly, Susan and I took a walk before tea to Bradford – Miss Mary Ostens came to Outchester with us – Susan went to Link Hall after tea and I took a walk with Miss Ostens. I went to the Low Mill to call on Nelly Davidson but she was from home. Mr Richardson came here to supper – a remarkable pleasant day.

Monday 4th

Mr Patrick Thompson and Mr Richardson called this morning. Yellowly Watson called before tea – weather the same as yesterday.

Tuesday 5th

I have been very busy today since eleven o'clock – flounced two petticoats, hemmed three yards of muslin, darned my sprigged muslin gown, made tea and last of all mended James' small clothes[21] – fine day.

Wednesday 6th

Bob Thompson drank tea here – I wrote to Miss Ronaldson – had a letter from Miss Dinning with our new hats from Newcastle – fine day.

Thursday 7th

Mr Walton called after tea – fine day.

---

[21] Knee breeches or underwear

Friday 8th

My Father is up at Newlands to see Mrs Dinning – I took a walk to Bradford – met Miss and Mr Maughan there – had on my new hat for the first time and unfortunately got a shower on the road – we have had several showers of rain and thunder.

Saturday 9th

Wrote to Susan – Mr Walton and I had a long tête a tête this afternoon – Susan came home from Link Hall tonight – been busy packing up my trunk for to be ready to go off on Monday – fine day.

Sunday 10th

Was at Belford church – after dinner I went up to Newlands – warm day.

Monday 11th

Wrote to Miss Dinning and answered a card I had from Harry which was sent me enclosing a silver pencil case – I went to Berwick to dinner – dined with my cousin Rankin – drank tea with Mrs Stevenson – made several calls – went to Old Cambus Town Head for supper – was there at nine o'clock – fine day.

Tuesday 12th

Town Head – took a walk over to Bowshiel to tea – very cold towards evening.

Wednesday 13th

Town Head – was at a sheep washing – dined at Town head – from there went to Bowshiel then to Blackburn with Miss Hoy to tea – walked four miles and returned to Bowshiel to supper – wrote to Miss Mary Wilson, Dunbar – a disagreeable wet day.

Thursday 14th

Bowshiel – Mr Landells of Coldingham called – Mr Bell of Dunglass came to dinner – had four beaux to tea – very wet.

Friday 15th

I took a walk over to Blackburn for my cousin Nelly – Mr Innes came to Bowshiel to dinner – and to escort us over to Town Head to meet a very large party – had an offer – but did <u>not</u> snap – stopped to supper – a very rainy evening.

Saturday 16th

Bowshiel – spent a dull day – went to Blackburn after tea – a fine day.

Sunday 17th

Miss Young came from Chapel Hill this morning after breakfast – I went to East Barns Meeting – fine day.

Monday 18th

Blackburn – went to Bowshiel to dinner – Chapel Hill to tea, called at Cockburnspath – fine day.

Tuesday 19th

Bowshiel – quite alone – fine day

Wednesday 20th

Bowshiel – was at the washing pool this morning – after dinner when I was sitting very composedly in my room, was rather a little astonished when a gentleman rushed in and threw a jug full of water in my face – I went out to see who it was – no sooner downstairs I was carried to a well, someone put me into it and kept me there, another took a can and poured water over me – had my dress to change – had a large company of old beaux to tea and supper – warm day.

Thursday 21st

Bowshiel – went to Hoprig to tea with my cousin Hood in the gig – could not return that night, it was so windy.

Friday 22nd

Hoprig – my cousin James escorted us to Bowshiel to dinner – I went to Town Head to tea – we took a walk to Mr Hay's cove – a very fine day.

Saturday 23rd

Townhead – dined at Bowshiel – drank tea at Blackburn – fine day.

Sunday 24th

Blackburn – went to Cockburnspath church, heard Mr Hume of Ayton preach – came to Chapel Hill to dinner – heard some very loud peals of thunder while we were in church.

Monday 25th

Blackburn – called at Bowshiel, came back to dinner – George Rankin was here – Miss Young and I went to Chapel Hill this afternoon, met Miss Hoy –

was at the bathing – went to Cockburnspath to tea – after tea we called at the Neuk, had a refreshment – a great number of gents came to Chapel Hill to supper – fine day.

Tuesday 26th

Chapel Hill – Miss Dods called us out of our beds this morning to go to the bathing at five o'clock – Miss Hoy was also with us – we got our breakfast at Linn Head with a bachelor – Miss Mary Wilson and I called at Bowshiel – from there went to Blackburn where we met a very large party from Dunbar – I came back immediately after dinner as I was engaged to go to Mrs Atchison's of Cockburnspath – met with some friends there – got a present of a pair of Habit gloves, a penknife and a pound of peppermint drops – I was mounted on an elegant horse today – remarkable fine day.

Wednesday 27th

Bowshiel – went to the Cove to tea – expected to have an excursion on the water – but was disappointed, the weather was so stormy – called at Linn Head – a very unpleasant day.

Thursday 28th

Bowshiel – a great party of ladies and gentlemen came here this afternoon – quite unexpected – this was Drill day for the 4th troop of East Lothian Cavalry – most of the beaux were in uniform – Doctor Turnbull assisted me to make a watch chain – we had a dance to vocal music – Miss Young and my cousin Nelly stopped here all night – I had a baking of shortbread today – heard from Outchester – fine day.

Friday 29th

Bowshiel – Miss Young, my cousin Nelly and Grace of Bowshiel went over to Townhead to dinner – I returned to Bowshiel, Agnes and Mrs Innes went to Butterdean Mains with me – we met some of our friends – Mr Innes and my cousin escorted us to Blackburn – Mr Innes stopped all night – fine day.

Saturday 30th

Blackburn – Miss Young went away this morning at 7 o'clock – Mr Innes went after breakfast – I have not been in such low spirits this month as I am today – I came over to Bowshiel after tea – got in better spirits towards evening – prepared my dress for the Meeting tomorrow – a very pleasant day.

July

Sunday 1st

Bowshiel – went to East Barn Meeting, came home in tandem – rainy day.

Monday 2nd

Bowshiel – called at Townhead – came in the Union coach to Berwick – dined at Mrs Wilson's – drank tea at Doctor Stevensons – supped there – slept at Mrs Wilsons – made several calls today – weather changeable.

Tuesday 3rd

Berwick – got my breakfast with Mrs Wilson – dined with Mr Stevenson – drank tea with Miss Redpeth, escorted home by Captain Ellis and Lieutenant Forbes – rainy day.

Wednesday 4th

Berwick – got my breakfast with Mrs Wilson – went to Lamberton races with Miss Bell from Newcastle and Mrs Bouch. Four ladies assisted me to dress for the Assembly – went in Mrs Clounie's party – danced with Lieutenant Guthrie – a very pleasant day.

Thursday 5th

Berwick – went out to the races with Mr & Mrs Todd – dined with Mr Todd and then dressed to go to the play with a large party – Mr Wilson treat me to the play which was 'The Tragedy of Douglas'[22] – a fine day.

Friday 6th

Berwick – got a pair of gloves from Lieutenant Pool – I bet with Mr James Baird and won – on Wednesday was at the play with Miss Bell – the comedy of 'She Stoops to Conquer' was performed.

Saturday 7th

Berwick – I made a great number of calls today – I got a pair of gloves from Mr Martin – a bet I made with him that Lord Belhaven's horse would win – got a present of a very handsome fan from Mr Thompson of Scremerston. Nichol came into Berwick for me – we supped at Elwick – no visitors have been at Outchester since I went away, but Miss Bawtree, Mr & Mrs Dinning, Mr Thompson and Doctor Turnbull.

---

[22] First performed in Edinburgh in 1756, it became a standard repertory piece

Sunday 8th

Mr Harry Dinning and Miss Dinnings called after tea – fine day.

Monday 9th

Went up to Newlands to tea – took a walk to West Hall, saw Mrs Trotter there, Miss Bawtree came to Belford with us – a very fine day.

Tuesday 10th

Quite alone – fine day.

Wednesday 11th

Mr Walton & Miss Walton called – I was at the bathing – had young potatoes to dinner the first time this season, disagreeable cold day.

Thursday 12th

Had green peas to dinner for the first time – the currant berries are ripe – bad crop of strawberries – fine day.

Friday 13th

Was at the bathing[23] this morning before breakfast – a very fine day.

Saturday 14th

Mr Steven Thompson called – John Younghusband came here to tea – I was at the bathing – a very fine day.

Sunday 15th

Susan and I were at Warenford Meeting, my cousin of Link Hall dined here – I went to Elford to tea – a fine day.

Monday 16th

Had a letter from Mrs Todd – Doctor Cockayne drank tea here – fine day.

Tuesday 17th

Took a walk to Newlands after dinner – from there to Belford – drank tea with Mrs Bromfield – Mr Walton called – a remarkable warm day.

---

[23] At Budle bay

Wednesday 18ᵗʰ

Met Mr Watson going to the bathing this morning – I went up to Waren with him – saw Mrs Sam Bawtree and Miss Charlotte Handyside – Mr Dinning called – fine day.

Thursday 19ᵗʰ

Quite alone – a thick fog.

Friday 20ᵗʰ

Was up at Newlands this afternoon – was regaled with strawberries and cherries – Miss Smith and Mrs Dinning arrived just before we sat down to tea – Barbara came down to Outchester – I escorted her home again – a fine day.

Saturday 21ˢᵗ

Miss Watson called after tea – fine day.

Sunday 22ⁿᵈ

James and I were at Warenford Meeting – from there went to Link Hall to dinner – rode out this afternoon – saw many gentlemen's seats – refreshing showers this morning.

Monday 23ʳᵈ

Miss Dinnings and Miss Smith drank tea here – fine day.

Tuesday 24ᵗʰ

Susan, Nichol and James were at Elwick – fine day.

Wednesday 25ᵗʰ

Mr Dinning called this morning – fine day.

Thursday 26ᵗʰ

Mr Dinning called and Mr Ross came to dinner – James, Susan and I went to Bambro' Castle to see Miss Maughan – we called at the Friars on our return – warm day.

Friday 27ᵗʰ

Miss Dinnings and Miss Smith called – I walked up as far as the turnpike – warm day.

Saturday 28th

Susan, James and I went up to Newlands this afternoon – after tea we took a walk to West Hall – Miss Bawtree came so far home with us – a fine day.

Sunday 29th

James went into Berwick today – he is to be in for a week with the rest of the troop on permanent duty – Mrs Weatherly came to dinner – Susan and I went over to Newham Newhouses with her where we met Mr John Fawcus and his father and Mr Ostens – from there I went to Link Hall – met Miss Fawcus and Mr Dawson – fine day.

Monday 30th

Link Hall – went to Alnwick Fair – got a gown from Mr Young – a dart from Mr John Fawcus and a silk handkerchief from my cousin – called upon Miss Wilson – drank tea with Miss Younghusband.

Tuesday 31st

Link Hall – quite alone – fine day.

August

Wednesday 1ˢᵗ

Link Hall – my uncle Hood and my Father came for me to go home – my cousin Agnes and Mr Innes with my uncle came to Outchester last night – called at priest Davidson's house – got home to supper – a dull day.

Thursday 2ⁿᵈ

Mr Innes and my uncle left us immediately after dinner – Miss Dinning and Miss Smith called after tea – a fine day.

Friday 3ʳᵈ

Had a letter from Miss Margaret Younghusband enclosing one from James, desiring Susan and I to come into the Assembly[24] tonight we went in a chaise with Miss Y H – dined at Miss Younghusbands of the Wool Market – went to the ball at 10 o'clock – danced the 2 first dances with Mr Fenwick Compton – next with Lieutenant Tanner and last with Mr Tom Smith – slept at the Kings Arms – went to bed at 6 o'clock – disagreeable wet day.

Saturday 4ᵗʰ

Got up at nine o'clock – got my breakfast with Mrs Todd where I met a large party of gentlemen – got a second breakfast at the Inn with another party – made several calls – got a pair of gloves from Mr Vardy – came to Belford in the coach – dined and drank tea at Newlands. Miss Duncan[25] the actress was in the coach.

Sunday 5ᵗʰ

My cousin and I went up to Belford church – called at Newlands – took a walk after tea to the turnpike – met Miss Dinnings and Miss Bawtree – fine day.

Monday 6ᵗʰ

Went to Bradford to tea – called at the Low Mill – a showery day.

Tuesday 7ᵗʰ

Quite alone – a dull cold day.

---

[24] In Berwick
[25] Appeared in 'The Honeymoon' at Drury Lane in 1805

Wednesday 8th

Mr William Humble, Miss Sarah Redpeth, Miss Chisholm, John Younghusband and Miss Watson drank tea here – Miss R, Miss C and I called at Waren – we took a long walk after tea – a very agreeable day.

Thursday 9th

Susan and my cousin went to Link Hall – I was left at home – a pleasant morning but a very rainy afternoon.

Friday 10th

Mr Dinning called – the weather is very changeable just now – we have had several showers of rain today.

Saturday 11th

Mr John Younghusband, Mr Fenwick Compton and Mr Harry Dinning dined here – Miss Bab Dinning and Miss Mabon drank tea – the weather the same as yesterday.

Sunday 12th

We were all at Belford church today as there was no preaching at Warenford – my cousin Burrell dined with us – weather the same.

Monday 13th

My cousin, Susan and I went to Newlands to tea – took a walk to Belford after – the weather still the same – My uncle James of Hoprig and my cousin from Linn Head were at Outchester when we got home.

Tuesday 14th

My cousin and I took a walk to Bambro' Friars to tea to see Miss Redpeth – a showery day.

Wednesday 15th

My cousin from Link Hall dined here – weather the same as yesterday.

Thursday 16th

My uncle James and cousin of Linn Head went away just after breakfast – I was up this morning at six o'clock to bake muffins – was at the bathing – weather still showery.

Friday 17th

Miss Watson, Mr Walton, Mr Chatto Watson, Mr Houndson, Miss Dinnings and Harry called after tea – cold day. Mr Richardson came to supper.

Saturday 18th

Had a letter from Miss Watson and one from my cousin Hood of Bowshiel – rather cold day.

Sunday 19th

My cousin and I were at Warenford – Henry Dinning and Mr Houndson called – Mr May and John McDonald, John Younghusband and Mr Carnforth all supped here. Mr C stopped all night – I drank tea at Newhouses – was home at seven o'clock – fine day.

Monday 20th

Miss Bawtree and William Watson called this morning – I drank tea with Mr Walton at Spindleston – fine day. My cousin left us today – Nichol went to Berwick with her.

Tuesday 21st

Mr May and John McDonald called – Mrs Bawtree and Miss Watson, William and Chatto drank tea here – a fine day.

Wednesday 22nd

My father and Susan were at Bambro' Friars today – Mr Young and Mr Ostens came here to supper – the weather was so cold we were obliged to have the fire on.

Thursday 23rd

Went up to Newlands – from there to Belford Fair – drank tea at Mrs Bromfields – there was a large party there – Mrs Trotter of Middleton, Miss Nichol of Alnwick, Mr John McDonald and Mr Rea from London, Mrs Pringle, Mr H Dinning and Barbara, Mr Court, James, Susan and self – fine day.

Friday 24th

Miss Watson called, Mr Wastall and William Watson called – Miss Smith and Miss Barbara Dinning drank tea here – we began the harvest today – weather good.

Saturday 25th

I called at Waren this morning – went up to Newlands after dinner – met Mrs Trotter, Miss Nichol, Mr Court and Mr Bugg there – the Scotch shearers came home today – we took a walk to Belford before tea – weather pleasant but rather chill.

Sunday 26th

I was at Belford church – sat in the Elwick pew. Coming home from church I was for riding home behind Mr Walton – I got on to the horse, but it would not carry double, so I was obliged to dismount again – Mr Walton drank tea here – fine day.

Monday 27th

We went to Elford Feast to see Miss Mary Young. My cousins from Link Hall were there and Mr Young, Mr Ostens, Mr Wilkinson and his son – we stopped to supper – had a pleasant showery day.

Tuesday 28th

Mr Dinning and Barbara called morning – we went up to Belford after dinner – from there to Newlands where we met Mr Cook, Mr Rea and John McDonald – took leave of Mrs D and Miss Smith, they go off to Newcastle tomorrow – fine day.

Wednesday 29th

Mr Steven Thompson dined here – got a present of some apples from Bradford – very fine day.

Thursday 30th

Quite alone – fine day.

Friday 31st

James came in before dinner and said he had met Mrs Redpeth and Jane Humble and they had promised to come to Outchester to drink tea. So in the afternoon I posted off to meet them – I walked almost to Bambro' but could see nothing of them – I returned home very much disappointed for James humming[26] me – John McDonald called before dinner, came back to tea and stopped all night – fine day.

---

[26] Tricking

September

Saturday 1ˢᵗ

John McDonald went away immediately after breakfast fine day.

Sunday 2ⁿᵈ

James and I went to Belford church and Newlands to dinner - Miss Dinnings went with us to Link Hall to tea, where we met Mr & Mrs Pringle, Dr Turnbull &c – pleasant day.

Monday 3ʳᵈ

Wrote to Barbara Dinning – had an answer – had a card from Miss Wood – answered it – Mr Tom Alder and Mr John Younghusband called – I took a walk after tea to meet the Miss Dinnings – fine day.

Tuesday 4ᵗʰ

Miss Redpeth came here after dinner – her and I called at Waren house – Miss Younghusband, Miss Wood and John Y-h-d drank tea here – a remarkable warm day.

Wednesday 5ᵗʰ

Quite alone – this day has been warmer than any day we have had this summer.

Thursday 6ᵗʰ

Quite alone – rather cooler.

Friday 7ᵗʰ

Ditto – Ditto.

Saturday 8ᵗʰ

Ditto – Ditto.

Sunday 9ᵗʰ

James, Nicholas, Susan and I went to Bradford to tea where we met Harry Dinning – very warm day.

Monday 10ᵗʰ

I finished a little cap I have been making for Mrs Hood of Old Cambus Town – it has been my principal employment this past fortnight – fine day.

Tuesday 11ᵗʰ

Miss Dinnings called after tea – we escorted them great part of their way home – we met Mr Watson – Yellowly led his horse and he walked home with Susan and I. I was at the bathing this morning – fine day.

Wednesday 12ᵗʰ

Harry Dinning called.

Thursday 13ᵗʰ

Susan and I went to Newlands to tea – a very windy day.

Friday 14ᵗʰ

Quite alone – pleasant day.

Saturday 15ᵗʰ

I have hemmed half a dozen neck cloths today – the weather is warmer just now than what it has been this summer.

Sunday 16ᵗʰ

Was at Warenford Meeting – George Cornforth breakfasted here – the weather continues warm.

Monday 17ᵗʰ

Miss Dinnings, Miss Redpeth, Miss Bawtree, John and Yellowly Watson drank tea here – my cousin David of Butterdean Mains was also here – had a letter from Mr C.K[27] – fine day.

Tuesday 18ᵗʰ

Wrote to my cousin of Bowshiel and Mrs Hood of Old Cambus Town – fine day.

Wednesday 19ᵗʰ

My cousin went away after breakfast – I took a walk to Belford after dinner – called on Mrs Henderson – fine day.

Thursday 20ᵗʰ

Mr Walton called – windy day.

---

[27] Not identified – perhaps a secret admirer!

Friday 21st

Mr Luke Scott and Harry Dinning called – a disagreeable cold day

Saturday 22nd

Mr Cornforth and Mr Harry Dinning dined here – rainy day.

Sunday 23rd

John Younghusband and Mr Cornforth called. James went to Elwick with them to dinner – they came here to tea – Susan and Nichol were at Waren to tea – I called twice there but did not stop – fine day.

Monday 24th

Susan and I went to Newlands to dinner – we went in the gig with Barbara to Belford races – returned to Newlands to tea – Mr Trotter was there – also Mr Bugg, Mr Cook, Mr Joe Mole, James and Nick, my cousin William Weatherly &c – disagreeable wet day.

Tuesday 25th

Quite alone – very fine day.

Wednesday 26th

Mr Dinning dined here – Mr Steven Thompson came after dinner and stopped to tea – Mr Walton called and my cousin William Weatherly came to supper and stayed all   night – pleasant day.

Thursday 27th

Quite alone – fine day.

Friday 28th

Mr Gibson of Lesbury dined and drank tea here – we had the Kirn[28] tonight – had a pleasant dance – fine day.

Saturday 29th

James and I were at Mr Scott's Easington to tea – we called twice on Mr Yellowly but he was from home – very pleasant day.

Sunday 30th

I was at Warenford meeting – had a long walk after tea – weather rather pleasant – have not had a good pen this month.

---

[28] Dance to celebrate the Harvest home

October

Monday 1st

Quite alone – windy day.

Tuesday 2nd

Went up to Newlands after dinner where we met Mr Hounsam – Miss Bab, Susan and I took a walk to Belford – had a letter from Mr C.K. – pleasant day.

Wednesday 3rd

Quite alone – weather rather windy.

Thursday 4th

I took a walk to Spindleston after tea – Mr Walton drank tea here – fine day.

Friday 5th

Mr Dinning called - Richard Wood dined here – weather pleasant but still windy.

Saturday 6th

Susan, Nichol and I were at Warenford Meeting – pleasant day.

Sunday 7th

Susan and I took the sacrament for the first time – we dined with Mr Ross – rain towards evening.

Monday 8th

James, Susan and I went to Newham to tea – where we met my cousins of Link Hall – we called at Newham Newhouses – I had a letter from my cousin Hood – a letter from Miss Dinning and a card from Mr Hounsam inviting us all to a ball on the 18th – fine day.

Tuesday 9th

Susan and I went up to Newlands – spent a pleasant afternoon – Mr Walton and Mr Richardson called at our house – a remarkable fine day.

Wednesday 10th

Mr Richardson called while we were at breakfast – he came also in the evening and stopped to supper – Chatto Watson also called – pleasant day.

Thursday 11th

Quite alone – fine day.

Friday 12th

Susan and I called at Waren house to see John Watson who is very ill – we met Mrs Captain Watson and Miss Grey there – Miss Forster of Glororum drank tea here – William Humble supped here –fine day.

Saturday 13th

Wrote to Miss Dinning – got an answer – Mr Blacketer and his son and Chatto Watson dined with us – Mr B stopped all night – Miss Bawtree and Miss Watson called this morning – fine day.

Sunday 14th

Nichol and I went to Mr Thompson's Meeting – William Weatherly came to Outchester to dinner – Nick and I went with him to Newhouses to tea – the weather continues very pleasant.

Monday 15th

Wrote an answer to Mr Hounsam's card saying we will come to the ball on Thursday – showery day.

Tuesday 16th

Miss Dinnings, Mr H Dinning, Mr John Dinning from Edinburgh and Mr Bugg drank tea here – Mr Housnam called – Mr Richardson came after tea and stopped to supper – very fine day.

Wednesday 17th

Doctor Pringle called – Susan and I went to Waren House to tea – disagreeable day.

Thursday 18th

Mr J Dinning and Babra' called this morning – we took a walk so far up with them – met with Mr Watson – Mr & Miss Maughan, Miss Ostens and Miss Jeffreys drank tea here – Mr Walton called – fine day.

Friday 19th

Susan and I went up to Newlands after dinner – from there with the Miss Dinning went to Belford to drink tea with Mrs Henderson – Mrs Bowes Smith was also there – rather cold day.

Saturday 20th

Mrs Bawtree and Miss Watson called – Susan and I took a long walk with them – a very fine day.

Sunday 21st

Quite alone – I was at Warenford – very rainy day – Mr Hounsam called.

Monday 22nd

William Watson came here to breakfast – Miss Dinnings, Harry and their cousin John dined and drank tea – disagreeable wet day.

Tuesday 23rd

Mr Clounie of Berwick called this morning – Mr Ostens and Mr Young also called – Mr Walton came here to tea – had a game at Whist – fine day.

Wednesday 24th

Quite alone – fine day.

Thursday 25th

John Younghusband called this morning – pleasant day.

Friday 26th

James and I took a ride to Elwick – called at Waren House – came to Newlands to supper – stormy day.

Saturday 27th

Wrote a card to Mr Hounsam – Mr JamesTrotter and his sister, and Mr Turnbull and his sister & Mr Smith dined here – cold day.

Sunday 28th

Susan and I went up to Newlands immediately after breakfast – Bab Dinning and I went to Belford church, returned to Newlands – stopped to dinner, tea and supper.

Monday 29th

My Father went to Scotland this morning – Susan and I went to Bradford to tea – cold day.

Tuesday 30th

Wrote to Miss Watson – Mr Yellowly called – cold day.

Wednesday 31st

We all went up to Newlands – from there to Wandylaw where we had a pleasant dance – I came to Newlands all night – fine day.

November

Thursday 1st

Newlands – Bab, Mr Jobling and I took a ride by Belford – came to Outchester – then I went alone to Chester Hill to see Mr Yellowly and Miss Watson – Miss W came home to dinner along with me – after tea Harry Dinning, his cousin and Mr Jobling called – they stopped to supper – I went to Newlands that night to be ready to go to Alnwick the day following – wet day.

Friday 2nd

Barbara and I set off for Alnwick immediately after breakfast – we went to Mr Wilsons – Miss Carples and Miss Wilson came to Newlands along with us – we called at Link Hall – we were at Newlands before dinner – our family were all up here – Mr Trotter, Laird Anderson &c &c – we had a dance – danced six couples – we stopped to supper – wet day.

Saturday 3rd

Mr William Watson called – Miss Watson came over to dinner – she spent the day with us. Mr Cornforth came from Alnwick along with James – weather rather pleasant.

Sunday 4th

Mr Richardson came here to breakfast and spent the day – My cousin Tom Weatherly of Hoprig and Mr William Blackadder came to dinner – Mr B and Mr Cornforth went away after tea – cold day.

Monday 5th

Mr Yellowly Watson called with a long letter from Margaret – I returned an answer – Miss Dinnings, their brother & cousin, Miss Wilson, Miss Carples, Mr Jobling, Doctor Trotter and Mr Walton drank tea here – we were sixteen all together – my cousin and Mr Blackadder included – fine day.

Tuesday 6th

Mr Yellowly Watson and Mr Blackadder drank tea with us – William went away with his father – fine day.

Wednesday 7th

Quite alone – fine day.

Thursday 8th

My cousin James and I were out hunting with the greyhounds – went to Link Hall to dinner – a very rainy afternoon.

Friday 9th

Mr Harry Dinning and his cousin John called this morning – fine day.

Saturday 10th

My cousin Thomas went away after breakfast – won two shillings at Lieu this week – John Younghusband came here to his supper – had a busy day baking – weather rather pleasant.

Sunday 11th

Was at Warenford Meeting today – Susan and I took a walk to Spindleston after dinner – a pleasant day but rather cold.

Monday 12th

Miss Mary Humble called this morning – Yellowly Watson and Harry Dinning also called – Susan and I went up to Newlands to tea - met Mr Pinkerton there – I wrote to Lieutenant Younghusband – a remarkable pleasant morning, rainy evening.

Tuesday 13th

I have been busy today cutting out chemises – I cut a dozen – wet day.

Wednesday 14th

Mr William Watson called this morning – after dinner Susan and I went to Chester Hill - met there Mr Housnam, Miss Bawtree, Miss Watson, William and Yellowly – had a hand at cards after tea – William and I against Miss Bawtree and James – we played six games – neither lost nor won – I lost sixpence by betting with Yellowly and a shilling to Susan – wet day.

Thursday 15th

Mr Walton came here to tea – played at cards, he and I against my Father and James for a penny the rubber – had a letter from Miss Dinning – I wrote up to Newlands – cold day.

Friday 16th

Mr John Younghusband called this morning – fine day.

Saturday 17th

Was at Spindleston Mill at a christening – Mr Thompson and Mr Richardson drank tea – Mr William Weatherly came to supper – weather still good.

Sunday 18th

Was at Warenford Meeting – fine day.

Monday 19th.

Had a letter from Miss Maughan – Miss Dinning and Mr Bromfield drank tea here – fine day.

Tuesday 20th

Miss Younghusband called this morning. Mr Lonsdale came to dinner, and Mr Todd of Berwick came after tea and stopped the night – Mr Todd and I were partners at cards, played against my Father and Susan – neither lost nor won – pleasant day.

Wednesday 21st

Susan and I went up to Newlands after dinner (the Colours were presented to the Glendale Troop today by Lady Haggerston) – we began immediately to dress for the ball at Chillingham Castle – the chaise came for the Miss Dinnings and us at 6 o'clock – we called at Chillingham Barns for Mrs Younghusband as we went in her party. We went into the room at nine o'clock – was introduced to Lady Haggerston – danced the first two dances with John Younghusband – next with Mr Tom Smith, next with Mr Johnston – then with John Hardy and last with Mr Robert Forster. There were between two and three hundred people at the dance – kept it up until 6 o'clock in the morning – arrived at Newlands for breakfast at 8 o'clock – remarkable pleasant day.

Thursday 22nd

Newlands – got up at half past two o'clock – Mr Young and Mr Trotter dined at Newlands – we as usual stopped until evening – Mr Y and Mr T called at Outchester – weather uncommonly fine.

Friday 23rd

Mr William Blackadder came here to dinner – we played at Lieu after tea – he and I were partners – won two shillings and four pence – fine day.

Saturday 24th

Quite alone – fine day.

Sunday 25th

James and I were at Belford church – Harry Dinning treat us with milk punch – after dinner James, Susan, Nichol and self went over to Chester Hill to see Miss Watson – met Miss Bawtree and William Watson there – Mr Richardson called just as we were going to bed – had a letter from Robert Younghusband, Dublin – fine day.

Monday 26th

Mrs Bawtree called this morning – we were all at Newlands to dinner – Harry Barber came there to tea – we stopped to supper – Mr Walton was at Outchester – fine day.

Tuesday 27th

Mr Trotter of Newham came here to breakfast – James, Nichol, Susan and I went to Mr Waltons to tea where we met Harry Dinning, Mrs Bawtree, William Watson and Margaret. Miss Watson and H Dinning called at Outchester – disagreeable day.

Wednesday 28th

Miss Watson called on us to go to George Grays at Spindleston Mill, where we met Mrs Bawtree and William Watson. My cousin Joseph Burrell from London – Nelly came to take leave of us before she went to London with her brother – weather still very unpleasant.

Thursday 29th

My cousins left us after breakfast, Mr Blackadder came to dinner – this is Miss Younghusband's wedding day – weather the same.

Friday 30th

Miss Dinnings and Mr Taylor of Fleetham came here to tea – we played at cards – I had Mr Taylor for a partner – won a shilling – had a letter from Miss Watson – unpleasant day.

December

Saturday 1st

John Younghusband called this morning and returned with James from Alnwick to tea – Miss Watson and Yellowly, Mrs Bawtree and William Watson were also here – John Younghusband stopped to supper – a pleasant morning, rainy evening.

Sunday 2nd

James and I went to Warenford – I took so ill after I was there, I could not go into the Meeting but had to go to bed. James, Susan and Nicholas were at Newham Newhouses this afternoon – a drizzling wet day.

Monday 3rd

Had a letter from Miss Watson and one from Bab Dinning – frosty day.

Tuesday 4th

Went up to Newlands after dinner to go to the first subscription ball. Miss Anderson, Miss Dinnings, Susan and I went all in one chaise. Led into the room by Mr George Selby – danced the first two dances with John Younghusband – then with George Selby, Joe Mole, William Watson, Patrick Mole and Captain Humble. Mrs Bawtree sung some songs after tea – returned as we came – very hard frost.

Wednesday 5th

Newlands – spent a pleasant day talking over the ball – Mrs Bawtree came after tea to take leave - I wept – have been very unwell today – sick to death – unpleasant wet day.

Thursday 6th

Had a letter from Harry Dinning – answered it – fine day.

Friday 7th

Quite alone – won a shilling at cards – weather still the same.

Saturday 8th

Was at Belford this afternoon – went to Newlands to tea – fine day.

Sunday 9th

Was at Warenford Meeting – a very rainy disagreeable day.

Monday 10th

Mr Young and Mr Ostens called this morning – we all went to Newhouses to dinner – played at cards – won two shillings – unpleasant wet day.

Tuesday 11th

Wrote to Miss Watson – William Watson called this afternoon – William Weatherly came here to dinner and stopped all night – fine day.

Wednesday 12th

Mr Wilson from Berwick came last night and went from here after breakfast – Susan and I dined at candle light – Mr Walton came to tea Mr Dinning called twice – very fine day. I spent this forenoon with Miss Watson at Chester Hill.

Thursday 13th

Had a letter from B.D – wrote to Miss Watson – Susan and I went up to Newlands – went with Miss Dinnings to a tea drinking one of the hind's wife had – spent a pleasant evening – fine day.

Friday 14th

Quite alone – fine day.

Saturday 15th

Miss Dinnings and Mr Walton drank tea here – tolerable weather.

Sunday 16th

Quite alone – very wet rainy day.

Monday 17th

James and I went into Alnwick – dined with Mr Wilson where we met Miss Sarah Anderson, Miss Atkinson, Miss Cashels – came to Link Hall to tea. Mr Thompson called while we were away – a very stormy day – intense frost, hail.

Tuesday 18th

Yellowly Watson breakfasted here – Mr Trotter of Newham called – hard frost.

Wednesday 19th

Mr Watson called – I wrote to Miss Dinning – had a letter from her – I wrote a long letter after the rest were all gone to bed – fine frosty day.

Thursday 20th

Quite alone – frosty day.

Friday 21st

I took a walk to Chester Hill this morning to call upon Miss Watson but she was from home – wrote to Mr John Wilson in answer to a letter I got from him last week Miss Dinning came here to tea on foot – a very fine day.

Saturday 22nd

Was up at 6 o'clock this morning – quite alone – unpleasant day.

Sunday 23rd

James and I went to Warenford – we took a walk to Spindleston after dinner – stormy morning, better afterwards.

Monday 24th

Susan and I went to Chester Hill to see Miss Watson who has got herself very much burnt – Susan went home to dinner but I stopped until eleven o'clock at night – met there Miss Mary Ann Gray and Mrs Watson, Mr Joseph Watson and Mrs Adams – pleasant morning, rain afterwards.

Tuesday 25th

Quite alone – fine day.

Wednesday 26th

Mr Walton called this morning – James and I went to Newlands to tea – called at Chester Hill and Belford – weather rather stormy.

Thursday 27th

William Watson called this morning – Mr Allison and his son Tommy were here to dinner – Mr Watson came back to tea – cold day.

Friday 28th

Mrs Hall is here today making my leno[29] gown I got from London. Mr Walton came to tea – Mr Lonsdale and Mr W supped – fine frosty day.

Saturday 29th

Miss Forster of Glororum called this morning – came back in the afternoon to tea – hard frosty day.

---

[29] Fine cotton material

Sunday 30th

Had a letter from Mr J Wilson – was at Belford church – Doctor Turnbull dined here – Susan and I took a walk after dinner to Chester Hill to see Miss Watson – we met Miss Dinnings and William Watson there – Mr Richardson called after supper – the frost is still very intense.

Monday 31st

Susan, James and I were at Glororum to tea – met Mr Cockayne, he was my partner at cards – won 10 shilling from betting at Whist – weather neither frosty nor fresh.

Begun this Journal for to improve my writing – now been scribbling at it for a year and still left room for improvement – will try what another year may do – I think this is the happiest year I have seen yet.

Interval

At the end of 1804 Eleanor wrote

'Began this journal for to improve my writing – now been scribbling at it for a year, and still left room for improvement – will see what another year may do. I think this is the happiest year I have seen yet.'

Unfortunately there was no transcript for another year. It seemed entirely possible that another transcript or even the original diary was mouldering away in an attic somewhere in the locality. Exhaustive enquiries proved frustratingly fruitless – all that remained was to complete the research into the later years of the family and bring the story to a conclusion.

Then amazingly some months later, a lady who had read an article of mine containing extracts from the diary, made contact. As a keen spinner and weaver she had been curious about some of the old terms used, and consequently put a query into a national journal for 'weavers'. She did receive some responses, but one in particular caught her attention. It came from a lady in Cumbria who couldn't help with the spinning terms, but asked where the extracts had come from, as they matched word for word with a diary in her possession.

What an unbelievable stroke of luck!

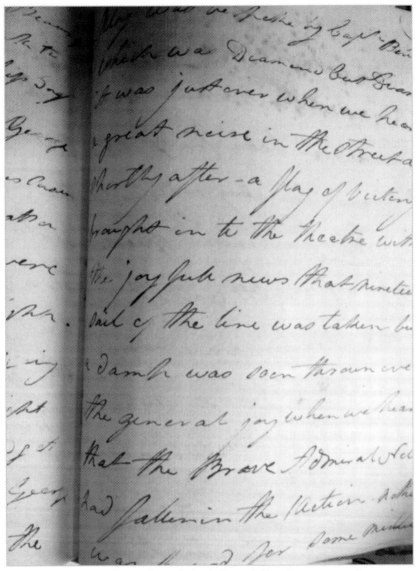

10: A page from the original diary following restoration

Interval

The diary owner was Elspeth Orrom, nee Oliver, whose family had lived for many years near Yetholm in the very north of Northumberland. The diary had been in that family's possession for over 100 years – and in fact it was Elspeth's mother who had typed out the copy for 1804 which had somehow found its way into the hands of Anthony Barber in north Northumberland.

What a thrilling experience to actually see and read the original diary – and a revelation for Elspeth to discover its provenance, for she knew nothing of this diarist, Eleanor Weatherly. Here too was the elusive diary for 1805, continued in the same volume, but not transcribed by Elspeth's mother.

Eleanor's Diary - 1805

January

Tuesday 1st

Mr John Younghusband and Miss Margaret Wood drank tea here, played at cards – won a few shillings – I sat up until one o'clock making a frill – weather frosty and pleasant.

Wednesday 2nd

After dinner I took a walk up to Newlands where I met Mr & Mrs Minton, Mr Jobling and Mr Windship – a remarkable fine day.

Thursday 3rd

Newlands – Barbara and I went to Mr Thompsons of Scremerston to dinner, where we met Miss Jonston of Elderton and her brother – from there went to Mungo Walls[30] to tea – had a very pleasant journey but the road was so slippery we were obliged to get out of the gig – saw a beautiful house at Ninewell Mill – the weather is very pleasant but no longer frosty.

Friday 4th

Mungo Walls – Barbara and I were sewing before we were out of bed – altering a gown for Bab to have on at the ball tonight – Mr James Thompson came here to dinner – we left the room after dinner to dress – Miss Harriots and their brother came to tea – Bab and I were dressed alike – had on white gowns with scarlet velvet sleeves – lace veils on our heads with a crescent and wreath of brown velvet leaves – we went into the ballroom at 8 o'clock – danced the first dance with Mr Sandy Thompson, then with Mr George Thompson, Mr Steward, Mr John & Mr Peter Cockburn, Mr Peter Tait, Colonel Brown then thrice with Doctor Trotter and Mr Robert Harriot. Danced reels with every gentleman in the room – I led off the New Claret which was quite new here and very much liked – I had two smart beaux at supper – never liked a dance so much as ever I was at – no dancing after supper which was at 4 o'clock – got home at 6 o'clock.

Saturday 5th

Got up to breakfast at eleven o'clock, having had a sound sleep – dreamed of nothing but the handsome Doctor Trotter. Bab, Sandy, George and I took a walk this morning to Swinoe – we got each a pair of gloves from George

---

[30] House near Duns in Berwickshire

who bet we could not walk so far after the dance. Called upon Mrs Whitelaw and Mrs Trotter of Broomdykes, who was staying at Dunse with Miss Davidson – I also called at Miss Youngs – went and saw the house that Mrs Trotter of Middleton has purchased – Doctor Trotter came to meet us – just as we finished dinner, in came Mr Robert Trotter and Captain Bell. Mr Adam Thompson and his son were here to dinner – after tea Mr Peter Tait came and insisted on stopping all night.

What a charming day this was – had dancing, singing and everything that could be thought of to give us pleasure. Forgot to say we had Robert Harriot and Miss Agnus Thompson to dinner – the beaux all stopped to supper – none of them but the Captain went home that night. Betsy Thompson and I went into Peter Tait's room after he was asleep – we wound up his watch and put a new string to it - pleasant, fresh weather today.

Sunday 6th

Mungo Walls – the beaux were not inclined to go to church, of course the ladies did not wish to go either. At breakfast it was proposed to go to the Crookses and see Mr George Thompson's house – the Doctor drove Bab and Betsy Thompson in the gig and I rode Mr Thompson's mare escorted by Mr David Murray and Mr Peter Tait – had Blackadder Burn to ride – very deep. Called at Mr Robert Harriots at Swinton Mill – got a glass of wine – viewed the house – saw a great many gentlemen's seats - Nisbett – Lord Swinton's at Hall Beck – Lord Humes at the Hirsell – Manderston – we rode up to the Hirsell Law, but the gig could not get up, as the Water Leet was not fordable, only for horses – I rode it up to the saddle laps –got whiskey punch at Crookses – biscuits and butter for a lunch – we next called at Mr Harriots of Spring Wells – where we saw the two Mr Slights. Then came to Bogend to dinner where we met Mr Robert Trotter, Miss Steward, Miss Moscrop and Mr Adam Thompson. Returned to Mungo Walls after supper – did not go to bed until we had a comfortable chat at the fireside - I was rather fatigued having rode above twenty miles before dinner – took leave of Mr Peter Tait which rather affected me – the weather is still fresh.

Monday 7th

Was quite melancholy this morning – did not wish to leave this enchanting country – Mr James Thompson of Bogend came to breakfast. The Doctor, Bab and I left Mungo Walls at the same time – George Thompson and the Doctor came so far on the road with us – Mr Thompson, Scremerston had to take charge of us through Berwick as the servant had taken the wrong road and missed us. I made some calls, paid an account for Miss Dinning – was at all the milliners shops in Berwick – walked about the street with Martin and a while with Miss Redpeth – called on a servant that once had lived with us – all in an hour – got a scold from Barbara for stopping so long. We dined at Scremerston – got to Newlands to tea where we met Miss Richardson and Mr Bugg and his son Compton, who danced a hornpipe four times over – rain this morning, afterwards pleasant.

Tuesday 8th

Newlands – went home to dinner – Mr Walton came to Outchester to tea – Mr Thomas Lawson, his brother David and Mr Richardson were at Outchester while I was from home – had a letter from Miss Watson – I went to bed at 7 o'clock – fine day.

Wednesday 9th

Wrote to Mr Richardson to set Mr Adam Trotter and Mr Thompson of Scremerston down for the subscribers to the Belford assembly. Mr Walton came to tea – I fell asleep and was obliged to go to bed – fine day.

Thursday 10th

Miss Dinnings and Miss Richardson came to tea – spent a very pleasant evening talking over the jaunt Bab and I had at Berwickshire – cold day.

Friday 11th

Mr Trotter of Newham called after dinner – he would not stop to tea – had a letter from Miss Watson, and Yellowly called twice – pleasant day.

Saturday 12th

Mr Walton called after dinner, he stopped all afternoon and to tea – had a game of cards, won 6 pence from him – wrote to Miss Watson – got an answer – fine day.

Sunday 13th

James and I went to Warenford Meeting – nobody was there but ourselves – so there was no preaching – we went to Newham Newhouses to dinner – wrote a card to Miss Mary Young and one to Mr & Mrs Trotter and Miss Richardson and one to my cousins at Link Hall – very stormy day.

Monday 14th

Quite alone – cold day.

Tuesday 15th

Nichol went off this morning to Blindyarn[31] on his way to Edinburgh – I went to Belford after dinner and then to Newlands to tea – had a rubber at cards – Mr Atkinson and I played against Bab and James – I lost 6d – pleasant morning – afterwards stormy.

Wednesday 16th

Mr Bromfield called this morning – rather pleasant day.

Thursday 17th

Had a card from Miss Mary Young. Mrs Trotter of Newham, Mr Ostens, Mr Dinning, Mr Atkinson, Mr & Mrs Pringle, Mr & Miss Young, Mr & Mrs Weatherly and little John all dined, drank tea and supped with us – we were all very merry – Mrs Trotter stopped all night – very fine day.

Friday 18th

Mr Young and Mrs Trotter breakfasted here – my cousin David Lawson came just as we finished dinner – fine day.

Saturday 19th

My cousin left us immediately after breakfast – Mr Watson came here to tea and stopped to supper – fine morning, stormy night. Miss Handyside & Miss Watson called.

Sunday 20th

James and I were at the Meeting – I wrote to Miss Ronaldson, Nichol and Miss Hamilton – the letters were to go in Nichol's trunk – disagreeable stormy day.

Monday 21st

Mr Richardson called this morning – Dr Turnbull from Dunbar came to spend a few days – I won 1/6 at cards – rainy day.

---

[31] Probably Blinarn near Duns, home of Mr Blackadder

Tuesday 22nd

We all went up to Mrs Bromfield to tea – we dressed there to go to the 2nd subscription ball – Miss Dinnings and Miss Sanderson called at Mrs B's for us – there were eight of us in the chaise. I danced the first dance with Dr Turnbull, then with Mr Johnston, Mr Patrick Mole, Mr Alexander Thompson, Mr John Younghusband, Lieutenant Sanderson, Laird Anderson, Mr Jobson – was engaged to Captain Coppin when we gave up – which was not until we were all completely tired. After the first 4 dances we changed partners every dance as there was a majority of eight gentlemen – danced 14 couples – did not get home until 8 o'clock.

Mr Bowlt[32] appeared at the ball with bridal favours, having married Miss Haggerston the day preceding to Sir Thomas Stanley. Miss Sarah Anderson was the handsomest girl in the room – we had supper which improved the gentlemen's dancing – this was the first dance I was ever tired with dancing at - a very stormy day.

Wednesday 23rd

Dr Turnbull, James, Susan and I went up to Newlands to dinner where we met Miss Anderson, the Laird and his brother, Mr William Barber, Mr Thompson of Scremerston, Miss Head, Miss Richardson and Mr Bugg. Harry Barber and the little Captain Cook were invited but could not come, they were so fatigued. Played at cards – the Laird and I against Miss Richardson and James – we won 6d – then joined the Commerce table where I won another 6d – stopped to supper. John Younghusband and his cousin Richard Wood were at Outchester while we were at Newlands – rather fine day.

Thursday 24th

Dr Turnbull left us this morning – had a busy day putting by my clothes and mending them – a remarkable fine day.

Friday 25th

Wrote to Miss Chisholm – John Younghusband and Richard Wood dined here – Miss Richardson and Miss Dinnings came to tea – Bab stopped all night – fine day.

---

[32] Vicar of Bamburgh

Saturday 26th

We went up to Newlands after dinner with Barbara – her and I went to Belford – we called on Mrs Barber – saw Cook in his uniform and heard him give the word of command – fine day.

Sunday 27th

Wrote to Nichol – very fine day.

Monday 28th

Mr Cook of Swinoe called – very drunk – cold day.

Tuesday 29th

Mr Walton came to tea – weather rather good.

Wednesday 30th

Quite alone – a stormy day, sleet and snow.

Thursday 31st

Wrote a card to Miss Watson – wrote to Nichol – the frost is very intense today.

February

Friday 1st

Miss Dinning, Miss Richardson, Miss Watson and William Watson dined and spent the day here – William hid Mary's fur tippet – never remember of laughing so much as I did this afternoon – tickling Mary Dinning's knees – had a present from Miss D of a preserved orange – fine hard frosty day.

Saturday 2nd

William Watson called this morning – I wrote to Robert Younghusband – John Weatherly of Butterdean Mains came to tea – cold stormy day.

Sunday 3rd

My cousin, James and I went to Belford church – Mary Anne Selby and I walked three times up and down the West Street – met with Captain Forbes – Mr Richardson dined with us – we went after dinner to Newham Newhouses – saw Miss Fawcus, Mrs Kerr, Captain Coppin – called at Spindleston – a very hard frost – had a card from Miss Anderson of Glanton.

Monday 4th

Mr Ostens called - wrote a very long letter to Nicholas and sent him 11/6d – we went to Newlands to tea where we met Mr & Mrs Trotter of Middleton, Mr Young and Mr Trotter of Newham – Miss Richardson is still there – Mr Y and Mr T escorted us home and called at Outchester – sleet and rain.

Tuesday 5th

Wrote to Miss Ronaldson and my cousin of Bowshiel – Mr Walton and Mr Heart came to tea – we played at cards – Mr H and I won 6d from my Father and Mr W – Mr H stopped all night – had a letter from Miss Ronaldson and Nicholas – coarse day, intense frost.

Wednesday 6th

My cousin John Weatherly left us after breakfast – we were all at Bradford to dinner where we met Mr & Miss Young, Mr Weatherly, Link Hall, Mr Watson, London. Played at cards after tea – I won a sixpence at Lieu – Mr Watson and I played at Whist against Miss Young and James – we won three shillings – stopped to supper – never spent a happier time at Mr Ostens – came home at 1 o'clock next morning – frost at the beginning of the day, fresh afterwards.

Thursday 7th

Wrote to Miss Dinning – got an answer – fine day.

Friday 8th

Mr Yellowly drank tea here – we played at cards – Mr Y and I against my Father and Susan – we lost sixpence – answered Miss Anderson of Glanton's card – fine day.

Saturday 9th

Miss Dinnings called here – we went to Newhouses to tea – James and I escorted them to Swinoe – we then came round by Elford and called upon Miss Mary Young – returned to Newhouses to supper – horrid roads to Swinoe – fine day.

Sunday 10th

John Younghusband came to tea – brought from Edinbro' a letter from Nichol and one to me from Miss Chisholm – had a letter from Miss Ronaldson – fine day.

Monday 11th

Yellowly Watson came to tea – he and I won a shilling from my Father and James at Whist – wrote to Miss Watson – fine day.

Tuesday 12th

Had a letter from Miss Watson – Miss Dinnings and young Sanderson of Swinoe, and John Younghusband called this morning – Mr Dinning called after dinner and three gentlemen, I don't know who they are – made the marmalade today – weather rather pleasant.

Wednesday 13th

Mr Ross came to dinner – Susan, James and I went to Elwick to tea – we stopped to supper – I won a shilling at cards – very fine day.

Thursday 14th

Went to Newlands to dinner where we met Mr & Mrs Trotter, Mr & Mrs Patterson, Mrs, Miss and John Younghusband, Mr Cook, Mr Mole and Mr Perrigle – we stopped to supper – won a shilling from Cook and Mole by betting.

Friday 15ᵗʰ

Mrs Hall and her apprentice were here today making a morning gown and pelisses – they stopped all night – fine day.

Saturday 16ᵗʰ

William Watson came here to breakfast – Susan and I went to Link Hall – we called with Mrs Weatherly on Miss Davidson of Charlton Mires – came home after tea – had a letter from Robert Younghusband – Miss Watson came here to tea but did not stop as we were from home – a remarkable fine day.

Sunday 17ᵗʰ

James and I were at Warenford Meeting and after dinner took a walk to Spindleston to call on Mr Walton. Miss Dinnings came down to Outchester but would not stop to tea, so we accompanied them to Newlands and drank tea with them – Barbara looks much handsomer than I ever saw her – a fine frosty day.

Monday 18ᵗʰ

Miss Dinnings and Miss Watson drank tea here – fine day.

Tuesday 19ᵗʰ

Had a letter from Nichol – quite alone – fine day.

Wednesday 20ᵗʰ

This being a Fast day[33] – James, Susan and I were at Belford church – a fine frosty day.

Thursday 21ˢᵗ

Mr Dinning called – Susan went to Mrs Trotters with Miss Dinnings – Mr Barber of Doddington dined and drank tea here – showery day.

Friday 22ⁿᵈ

Quite alone – fine day.

Saturday 23ʳᵈ

Mr Maughan called – Susan and I drank tea at Chester Hill with Miss Watson – William Watson came after tea – fine day.

---

[33] Ash Wednesday

Sunday 24th

I wrote to Miss Chisholm, Miss Mary Wilson, Miss Mary Lee, my brother Nicholas and Miss Ronaldson. Mr William Humble, Mr Gibson and Mr John Fawcus dined here – I went to Doddington to tea – met Miss Coppin there and Mr Laidlaw of Chatton – very fine day.

Monday 25th

Doddington – Miss Coppin and I took a long walk before breakfast – Mr Archbold, Mr Harry Barber, Mr Gibson, Mr Fawcus, Mr T Barber dined. I won a shilling playing at Lieu and seven shillings at Whist – a fine day rather frosty.

Tuesday 26th

Doddington – a gentleman bet me this morning a dozen pairs of gloves I would be married to John Younghusband – a guinea I will look plainer than I do now, six years hence – and half a dozen pairs of gloves I will be married in the space of two years – and another half dozen pairs of gloves if I am not married in six years time, I will never be married. Mrs Barber and Miss Coppin were witnesses to the bets. Left Doddington after breakfast – hunted all the way home, but we only got one hare – I set up two, but the dogs were not near – we called at Mr Snowdens and at Hetton House and at Mrs Barbers, Belford. Mr Sandy Trotter dined here – Miss Dinnings and John Younghusband came to tea – very fine day.

Wednesday 27th

Mr Young and William Weatherly drank tea and supped here – Mr Dinning called – Susan went off to Edinburgh this afternoon – fine day, rather cold,

Thursday 28th

Dr Turnbull dined here – pleasant day.

March

Friday 1st

Dr Turnbull dined here – very pleasant day.

Saturday 2nd

I went to Newlands this morning – while I was away Miss Watson wrote for me to take a ride to Newlands and Belford along with her, so I returned to Newlands to dinner – stopped to tea – a very fine day.

Sunday 3rd

James and I were at the Meeting and at Waren to tea where we met Miss Handyside, Miss Dinning, Captain Wallace – fine day.

Monday 4th

Miss Fawcus and Miss Forster of Glororum drank tea here – I won 3 shillings at cards – a windy day.

Tuesday 5th

I had a letter from Miss Watson – went to Newlands to tea – met there Miss Handyside, Mrs & Miss Watson – from there we went to Belford to see 'The Conjuror' and the players[34] – never saw as many beaux at Belford – they were five officers in the theatre – six – David Hunter Blair was one of them – came back to Newlands and stopped all night – fine day.

Wednesday 6th

Newlands – Miss Watson and I after we had breakfasted went to Belford – called at Mrs Hendersons, at Dr Herriots & Captain Humble – returned to Newlands to dinner – Miss Handyside, Miss Dinning, Miss Watson, Mr Walton were all at Outchester to tea – fine day.

Thursday 7th

Wrote a long letter to Susan – had a letter from Miss Watson – Mr Dinning called – had a letter from Susan – a very fine day.

Friday 8th

I went to Chester Hill today after dinner to call on Miss Dinning and Miss Watson to go to Mr Mole's Grainge – where we went to tea and met Mr Cook and Mrs Watson and Miss Handyside – we were all very merry – we

---

[34] Probably itinerant entertainers

83

played at cards – Commerce – I won the pool which was four shillings – the weather still continues remarkable fine.

Saturday 9th

Quite alone – fine day.

Sunday 10th

Mr William Barber of Boomer was here this morning before any of us were up – he spent the forenoon here – I wrote to Bab Dinning, Nichol and Susan – had a letter from Susan – I went to Newlands to tea this being Miss Dinning's Birth Day – we met Mr Richardson, and Mr & Mrs Pringle there – came home very early – fine day.

Monday 11th

Had a letter from Nichol and Susan. James and I were at Waren House to dinner where we met Mr Mole, Mrs Captain Wallace, Miss Dinning and Miss Handyside – after tea we played at Commerce – Miss Watson, Mole and Weatherly were in co. – we won the pool which was four shillings and sixpence – which was 1/6d each – we stopped to supper – I never remember seeing such a fine day at this season of the year – it was so warm and mild.

Tuesday 12th

Quite alone – fine day.

Wednesday 13th

Quite alone – fine day.

Thursday 14th

Mr Henderson of Newton and his son called – very fine day.

Friday 15th

Went up at Newlands after dinner where I met Major Hughes – a remarkable pleasant day.

Saturday 16th

Had a letter from Miss Lee – Mr Cornforth came here just as we were going to bed – he stopped all night – weather still very good.

Sunday 17th

Had a letter from Susan one from Nichol and part of one from Bab Dinning – I went up to Newlands this morning to call on Mary to go to church – after dinner I went to Newham Newhouses where I met Mr Watson, Mr Stables and Mr Tom Ostens – a remarkable fine day.

Monday 18th

After dinner James and I went to Newham. We called at Bradford, saw Captain and Mrs Wallace there – called Hoppen saw Miss Mary Humble – next at Newhouses for Miss Young. She accompanied us to Mr Trotters, Newham where we went to tea and from there to the play – we supped at Newham and called at Newhouses on our way home – fine day.

Tuesday 19th

I called at Chester Hill this morning on Miss Watson – Mr Trotter and Mr Davidson drank tea here – had a letter from Miss Maughan – a fine day.

Wednesday 20th

Mr & Miss Maughan, Mr & Miss Dinning & Miss Mary Humble drank tea here, cold day.

Thursday 21st

Mr John Ostens drank tea here – fine day.

Friday 22nd

Mr Richardson came to supper – had a letter from Bab Dinning – stormy day.

Saturday 23rd

Took a walk to Belford, called at Newlands and at West Hall and upon Miss Barber – had a letter from Miss Watson – she called upon me to go to Chester Hill – I went with her where I met Mr Joseph Watson – had a game at cards – Mr Yellowly and I against Mr Joe and Margaret. Mr Walton called here after dinner and William Watson called after tea – I got a present of a dog from Steven Thompson – fine day.

Sunday 24th

Mr Richardson came here to breakfast – I rode to Warenford Meeting alone – after dinner took a walk to meet Miss Dinning – I met her on the turnpike – Mrs Henderson came along with her to tea and after tea Mr Henderson called – I wrote until Monday morning finishing a letter to Bab Dinning and Susan which was twenty four pages long – also wrote to Nichol in answer to one I received from him today – fine day.

Monday 25th

Wrote to Miss Mary Humble and to Miss Young of Newham Newhouses – went up to Newlands to dinner where I met Mr Walton, Mr Forster, Mr Wales, Mr Barnett, Mr Watson and Mr Joseph and Yellowly – the Watsons went home before tea – but the rest of the company stopped all night – Mary and I slept on the sofa – very fine day.

Tuesday 26th

Newlands – the gents left us after breakfast – Miss Dinning and I went to Elwick to tea where we met Mr Mole, Mr Cook, Mr Fenwick Compton, Mr Wood and Mrs Younghusband of Ross – met with a deal of civility – we stopped to supper – very fine day.

Wednesday 27th

Newlands – went to Mrs Trotters to tea – Mary Dinning came to Outchester with me – Mr Stobbs and Mr Tom Ostens had been at Outchester today – the weather is remarkable pleasant and warm.

Thursday 28th

Mr Walton, Forster, Barnett and Wales called this morning – afterwards Mr Dinning and Mr Henderson – after dinner Miss Dinning and I took a walk to Bambro' – called at the Friars and at Dr Cockayne's – William Humble came to Outchester to tea with us – Mr Walton also drank tea here – a very fine day.

Friday 29th

Miss Dinning and I spent this day very comfortably by ourselves – she left me after tea – a very rainy morning but remarkable pleasant afternoon.

Saturday 30th

James and I went to Berwick – dined with Mrs Todd – drank tea with Mrs Stevenson – saw a great number of beaux – called upon Mrs Alan Shaw, Mr Rankin and Mrs Goodwill – rode from Berwick to Belford in an hour and a quarter – called at Newlands – rainy day.

Sunday 31st

Called at Newlands on our way to Warenford Meeting – was alone all afternoon as my Father and James are both at Newham Newhouses – dull rainy day.

April

Monday 1st

Wrote to Miss Dinning in answer to a letter I received from her this morning – had a letter from Bab Dinning honoured by Mr Sigan – wrote to Susan and Nichol – fine day.

Tuesday 2nd

Mr Dinning called – I went to Newlands to tea and got myself completely wet coming home as it was a very rainy evening – cut a dozen shirts for Nichol.

Wednesday 3rd

William Watson called before breakfast – before dinner and then after dinner – Mr Walton called after tea – we played a rubber at cards – I won sixpence – pleasant day.

Thursday 4th

Miss Watson came here to tea before 2 o'clock to assist me with my work – fine day.

Friday 5th

Had a letter from Bab Dinning which I answered – wrote to Miss Dinning – got an answer – had a letter from Miss Watson which she sent over with two pairs of wrists she had stitched for me – I wrote to her also – it has rained incessantly all day.

Saturday 6th

Wrote to Miss Watson and to Susan and Nichol – after dinner James and I took a walk to Belford – where we met Miss Younghusband and Mrs Younghusband of Ross – went to Newlands to tea – had a letter from Susan sent with her green gown and a pair of bibles – stopped at Newlands all night – fine day – had a letter from Miss Ronaldson.

Sunday 7th

Newlands – got downstairs to breakfast at 8 o'clock – John Younghusband came there to escort Miss Dinning and I up to Learmouth – we called at Wooler upon Miss Handyside – got to Mrs Comptons at 2 o'clock – a very pleasant day.

Monday 8th

Learmouth – after breakfast Mr & Mrs Compton[35] with Miss Dinning in the gig and John Younghusband on horseback went to take an airing – we went to Coldstream and Cornhill and got back home to dinner about 3 o'clock – we had just drunk tea when in came Mr Givens the fiddler – we danced until we were all tired – I sported a green lustre which was very much the worse of the excessive heat – fine day.

Tuesday 9th

Learmouth – John Younghusband, Miss Dinning and I took a walk to Preston to call upon Miss Woods – they accompanied us to Learmouth to dinner – Mr Givens played all over the new tunes – we had another dance – John Younghusband went away after tea – we had a game at cards , lost – fine day.

Wednesday 10th

Learmouth – my brother James came here after breakfast – Miss Woods stopped all night – Mr Givens is still here – I have made a bet with Mrs Compton that before this time twelvemonth she will have an addition to her family –we left this pleasant place after dinner and got to Newlands to tea – Mary was very cross on our way home – I got home to supper. Mr Grey of Swinoe was at Outchester when I arrived – very fine day. We have got our tickets for the next Belford ball – I wish we may have plenty of beaux but am rather doubtful.

Thursday 11th

Wrote to Miss Watson, Miss Dinning, Susan and Nichol – had a letter from my cousin of Bowshiel – Miss Dinning and Miss Thompson of Mungo Walls drank tea with me tonight – a very fine day.

Friday 12th

We are all very dull today having heard of the death of my Aunt Catherine – Mr Atkinson called – fine day.

Saturday 13th

Had a letter from Miss Watson – went to Belford this morning to buy Mourning – Mr Richardson came here to supper. I am in very low spirits as

---

[35] Mary Younghusband had married Fenwick Compton of Learmouth

my Father is so dull on account of the death of my aunt. I wish I may get to the ball next week – if I don't will be very much disappointed – weather uncommonly pleasant.

Sunday 14th

Had a letter from Nichol and Susan – I went up to the Belford Meeting – called on Miss Dinning – after dinner as I was taking a walk I met Miss Handyside and Miss Watson going to Newlands – I went up with them but did not stop to tea as my father was alone – very fine day.

Monday 15th

I intended to have gone with Miss Watson today to see Mrs Wallace, but the weather prevented us, as it has been raining since dinner time. Mr Walton and Mr Ostens called – have wrote to Susan and Bab Dinning – we had radishes to dinner yesterday for the first time this season – as I was walking today I met Oswald Younghusband – I can neither eat nor sleep thinking about the ball which is on Wednesday.

Tuesday 16th

Took a walk to Bradford for Miss Ostens who came here to tea – as so did the Miss Atkinsons of Ryle, Miss Sarah Anderson and Miss Dinning – we could talk of nothing but the ball. My Father had to go to Newlands so we were all very happy – a very pleasant day.

Wednesday 17th

Had a letter from Miss Dinning – went up to Newlands after dinner where I met Miss Anderson, Miss Sandersons, Miss Atkinsons, Captain Forbes – the ladies were all dressing when I arrived for the ball – we entered the room without a beau – I danced the two first dances with William Humble – next with Patrick Mole then Joe Mole – three dances with William Barber, Boomer and one with John Younghusband. We danced 10 couples and were all in great spirits – had an offer – got a letter from Susan in the ballroom – was dressed in a short blue gown with lace let in around the bottom – blue beads with brown net on my head – cord and tassel at waist, an inch long. Had only 7 country dances – every lady was in the room before any of the gents made their debut – there were 19 ladies and 26 gentlemen – gave up dancing at 5 o'clock – fine day.

Thursday 18th

Newlands – all the ladies took a walk to Belford escorted by Mr William Barber, Alnwick after dinner – Harry Barber, Mr Bugg, William Barber, Boomer, my brother James, Mr Patrick and Joe Mole came in – we danced until supper. Mary Dinning and I amused ourselves with knotting all the gents hats so they could not go home, and we sewed up the arms of Joe Mole's greatcoat – we had songs after supper – fine day.

Friday 19th

Newlands – I came home after breakfast – Mr Walton called here after tea – am not at all fatigued with dancing, but dull that all the balls are over – fine day.

Saturday 20th

John Younghusband came here to breakfast – after tea Miss Dinning and Miss Atkinsons of Ryle came here – not long after James and John Younghusband returned from the market – the ladies were very much wet with the rain as it has been a shower, but now is fair weather – wrote to Susan – fine day.

Sunday 21st

Went to Belford church – from there to Newlands – Miss Dinning, the two Miss Atkinsons and I in the gig – Mr Richardson stopped there until 8 o'clock – Mr R came to Outchester to supper – fine day.

Monday 22nd

I took a walk to Chester Hill after tea – met Mrs & William Watson, Mr Ostens, Mr Walton. William and Miss Watson called here – the weather is rather cold.

Tuesday 23rd

Quite alone – cold day.

Wednesday 24th

Mr Hobbs called – had a letter from Miss Watson – answered it – had several showers of rain today.

Thursday 25th

Wrote to Miss Dinning – had an answer – Miss Watson wrote for me to come to Chester Hill – I went – met Mr Joseph Watson there – showery day – Mr Watson supped here.

Friday 26th

Had a letter from Susan honoured by Mr Tom Logan – answered it – had a letter from Miss Dinning for me to go to Ross with her – my Father would not let me go – I have been very dull today as I see by the papers that Robert Younghusband is sailed for the East Indies –disagreeable day.

Saturday 27th

Had a note from Miss Watson sent over with a shirt she had sewed for me – after tea I took a walk to Newlands – Mary and I had a pleasant chat – she accompanied me home a great part of the way – wrote my cousin of Bowshiel – the weather is much colder than it was some weeks ago.

Sunday 28th

I went to Newham Newhouses to tea – very cold day.

Monday 29th

Miss Watson called this morning – we had a long walk. She went home and came back here to tea – we went to Spindleston to see the improvements in Mr Richardson's house – Mr Steven Thompson called – fine day, but rather cold. I finished the dozen shirts I began this month.

Tuesday 30th

I walked to Elwick this morning and from there to Belford – John Younghusband went there with me – I then met Miss Forster who came home with me – we got to Outchester to dinner – I called on Mrs Herriot – Miss Dinning drank tea here – fine day. Mr Walton was here – I won two pence at cards

May

Wednesday 1st

After dinner I took a walk to Newlands – about 6 o'clock the party arrived from Edinbro' – Nichol is a great buck – speaks fine, has a stock up to his nose – Susan and Barbara dressed in velvet pelisses[36] look quite stylish – the noise we made was ridiculous – Mr Bugg and Mr Anderson from I can't tell where, was there - had a letter from Miss Watson with a present of a pen cleaner – had a letter from Miss Chisholm and my cousin of Bowshiel – showers of snow – cold.

Thursday 2nd

Quite alone – cold day.

Friday 3rd

Miss Watson called – the weather is rather warmer.

Saturday 4th

Susan and I were at Warenford Meeting – we called at Bradford on our return home – a servant came for us, saying that Mr Compton, Mr Walton and Mr John Younghusband were come to Outchester to tea – they stopped to supper. Mr Richardson called – we were rather fatigued as we walked to the Meeting – fine day, cold.

Sunday 5th

The whole family were at the Meeting – this being the Sacrament day – we dined with Mr Ross – Mr Johnston of Wooler came home with us and stopped all night – a showery day.

Monday 6th

Nichol and I went to the Meeting to hear Mr Johnston preach – was at John Johnston's funeral today – Mr Sanderson just dined and drank tea here – showery day.

Tuesday 7th

William Watson called – Mr & Mrs Trotter of Middleton with Miss Dinnings drank tea with us – weather changeable.

---

[36] Edge to edge coat, usually calf length

Wednesday 8th

After dinner I took a walk to Belford – and drank tea at Mr Steven Thompsons – when I came home, Mr Thompson the clergyman was here – weather still the same.

Thursday 9th

Susan and I after breakfast took a walk to Elwick to call upon Mrs Compton – John escorted us home – called upon Miss Watson at Chester Hill – Miss Forster of Glororum drank tea here – Miss Watson called after tea as did Mr Walton – the weather changeable and disagreeable.

Friday 10th

Nichol and I went to Link Hall to dinner – from there to Alnwick – did a great deal of business and to Bassington to tea – the first time I have been to see Mrs Nichol Burrell – had a long letter from Miss Watson – got several showers of rain.

Saturday 11th

Bassington – we came away after breakfast – called at Link Hall – got home to dinner – Miss Watson called upon us to go to Newlands –when we were half way on the road a shower of rain came upon us which wet us to the skin – we walked to Belford after tea and called on Mrs Barber – the weather is colder and more stormy than it was a month ago,

Sunday 12th

James, Nichol and I were at Warenford Meeting – Nick, Susan and I went to Bradford to tea – we were home before 7 o'clock so took a walk to Chester Hill – Mr Ned Smith and William Watson were there – the weather is very changeable.

Monday 13th

I took a walk to Spindleston after dinner – fine day.

Tuesday 14th

Have been very dull today – weather still changeable.

Wednesday 15th

Had a large party to dinner – Mr & Mrs Compton, the Younghusbands of Elwick, the Dinnings, Miss Watson. Mr Mole &c - Captain Humble came to supper – disagreeable wet day.

Thursday 16th

Miss Watson slep't with us last night, she left us after breakfast – we were all at Newlands to dinner where we met the Elwick family, Mr & Mrs Compton, Mr & Mrs Cook, William Watson and Joe Mole – Mrs Compton was smartly dressed in a bloom sarsanet – drooky day, Tony Barber called at Outchester.

Friday 17th

Had a letter from Miss Watson – answered it – Mr Walton and William Watson were here to tea and supper – had a rubber at Whist – William and I against my Father and Mr Walton – I won sixpence. Had two bowls of punch to drink Nichol's joy – he leaves Outchester tomorrow – I wrote to my cousin Burrell, to Captain Renton, to my cousin at Bowshiel – it was after two o'clock before I got to bed. Nichol was writing to a friend but the punch had been too potent for he missed a page in his letter – dull day.

Saturday 18th

Nichol left us this morning – we were all very sorry to part with him – James has gone to see him on board – dull morning but most delightful evening – a letter from Miss Watson.

Sunday 19th

Susan and James went to Newham Newhouses to tea and left my Father and I quite alone – the weather is very disagreeable.

Monday 20th

John Younghusband came here after tea – he stopped to supper – he told us that Mr Werges with James and him, saw Nichol over the Bar at Berwick on Saturday – Mr Joseph Watson called – a dull misty day.

Tuesday 21st

We went to Newlands to tea where we met Miss Tombling, Miss Carnforth, Mrs Henderson and Mrs Scott – spent a very pleasant evening – fine day

Wednesday 22nd

Miss Dinnings were here to tea – I went to meet them – went a good deal out of our way to put up some of Mr Weddel's fat sheep which were laying awkward – the weather is dull and cold.

Thursday 23rd

Mr Ostens called – my Father is very anxious to hear about Nichol – he is often looking out to see if the weather is fair – this has been a misty cold day – north wind.

Friday 24th

Susan and I took a walk to Chester Hill to see Miss Watson after dinner – we called at Spindleston upon Mr Walton and from there to Glororum to tea, where we met Mrs Cook and we had a long chat about the Bent Hall dance – after tea we went to Bambro' Friars and likewise to the Castle to see Miss Maughan – then returned the way we came – pleasant day but cold.

Saturday 25th

William Watson was here to breakfast – Harry Dinning called afterwards. Mr Dinning called and said he would return to dinner – he came back at 2 o'clock – after tea I walked to Newlands from there to Belford – got a letter from Nichol, he got to London on Thursday morning – fine day.

Sunday 26th

My Father and I were at the Meeting – Mr Richardson dined and spent the day with us – fine day.

Monday 27th

After dinner Susan and I went to Newlands where we met Mr Handyside. Miss Dinnings went with us to Middleton sale – we got a dreadful fright with some cows that were in the field, as we had a dog with us which attracted their notice. They ran after us and had Mr Jobling not protected us we probably might have been hurt. Barbara tumbled over with fear, as the dog belonged to me, it got as close by my side as possible – and I was of course surrounded by cows – however we surmounted all difficulties and reached Middleton to tea, where we met several of our acquaintances viz the Detchant family, John Younghusband, Joe Mole, Mr & Mrs Cook, Mrs Patterson &c – we took leave of Mr & Mrs Trotter – William Humble was at Outchester to tea – fine day.

Tuesday 28th

We were at a bride's tea drinking – Mr Walton called – this is Belford Fair and we were not there – this is the first Belford Fair we have been absent from this ten years – the weather is very unpleasant and cold.

95

Wednesday 29th

Miss Watson called upon us as did Harry Dinning and Mr Jobling – after tea we walked up to Newlands – the Selbys of Detchant were there and Miss Hately. We had a pleasant sail in the boat – Mary Ann Selby wishes very much to go to the ball – James is to send her a ticket – this has been a pleasant day, but had a hearty shower this afternoon.

Thursday 30th

Miss Dinnings, Miss Hately, Harry Dinning, Mr Jobling and Mr John Fawcus drank tea here – this has been a very pleasant day.

Friday 31st

Miss Humble called upon me to go to Newlands along with her – I went and met Miss Bugg there. Miss Ds and I escorted Miss B to Belford – Miss Humble astonished us very much with speaking so fine – the weather is very changeable, this day is rather cold – had a ticket from William Humble for the Bent Hall ball.

June

Saturday 1st

Quite alone – fine day.

Sunday 2nd

Susan and I took a walk to Chester Hill to see Miss Watson – met Miss Dinnings and Miss Hately there – had a card from Miss Morton and one from Miss Ord – fine day.

Monday 3rd

Quite alone – fine day.

Tuesday 4th

Susan and I went up to Newlands as Miss Dinnings are by themselves – their father and mother having gone to Whitsome Bank fair – we spent a pleasant day – my cousin John Weatherly of Blackburn came from the fair with James and my Father – fine day.

Wednesday 5th

Went up to Belford after tea – called upon Mrs Scott and Mrs Henderson – Miss Watson called at Outchester – we were all from home – a pleasant day.

Thursday 6th

Had a letter from Miss Watson in answer to one I sent this morning – my cousin left us after breakfast – just going to dress to go to Swinoe and from there to the ball. We went to Swinoe – the Dinnings, Sandersons and us drank tea at Bent Hall – Joe Mole and John Younghusband drank tea at Outchester – went into the Assembly room at nine o'clock – danced with William Humble first then with Joe Mole – he and I led off the New Claret – then danced with Peter Mole, John Younghusband, Tom Sanderson, John Fawcus and Tony Barber – had a merry dance but rather confused. Harry Dinning, Joe Mole and John Younghusband came home with us to breakfast on……

Friday 7th

We did not go to bed – we reached home at 7 o'clock – fine day.

Saturday 8th

After dinner Mr Walton popped in, but James and I left him and took a ride to Easington – we drank tea there, came round by Belford from there and called at Newlands – fine day.

Sunday 9th

Was at the Meeting – a disagreeable cold day.

Monday 10th

John Younghusband called – fine day.

Tuesday 11th

Was up this morning between 5 & 6 o'clock to bake bread – baked as much bread as would last us ten days – Miss Dinnings, Miss Watson and Mr Walton called – had a very pleasant chat about Mr Richardson's marriage – fine day.

Wednesday 12th

Mr Dinning called – wrote to Nichol – this is the first letter I have sent to Horningsham[37] – took a walk to Newlands after tea, met Mr Taylor of Fleetham and his brother – pleasant day but rather cold.

Thursday 13th

Quite alone – fine day.

Friday 14th

Mr Dinning called this morning and came back to dinner – fine day.

Saturday 15th

I forgot to say yesterday that I took a walk to Bradford – it was after their tea hour, but before we had thought of getting tea at Outchester – Miss Dinning and Miss Watson called after tea – a pleasant day, had a refreshing shower in the evening.

Sunday 16th

Susan and I were at Belford church – saw a great number of officers – Mr Richardson spent the day with us – this is the last visit he will make here

---

[37] Near Longleat House, Nichol was probably apprenticed there.

until after he is married – Susan and I took a walk to Waren House – a very pleasant day.

Monday 17th

Had a letter from Miss Watson – went up to Newlands to tea where we met Miss Sandersons of Swinoe wih their father, Mr Bugg, & Mr Walton – it was pouring of rain when we returned home – William Watson overtook us – we were wet to the skin – I never remember of being out in such a wet night.

Tuesday 18th

Had two wool buyers to tea – William Watson called and brought me a pair of gloves – after tea Joe Mole and Margaret Watson called – Joe was in his usual high spirits – we took a walk with them – had a talk about the ball which is to take place on Friday – fine day.

Wednesday 19th

Had a letter from Miss Watson and wrote to Bab Dinning – got an answer – wrote also to Margaret Younghusband and got an answer. Mr Richardson of Spindleston is taken unto himself a wife today – had three chaises at the wedding – the happy party dined at Holy Island. William Watson came here to tea – George Carnforth came after tea & gave us a full and particular account of the wedding – he stopped here rather too long and when he returned to the Bride's party, could not gain admittance, so he had to return here to sleep – fine day but rather cold.

Thursday 20th

I have been since Monday working at my ball dress – it is now finished. Mr Ross dined here – Mr Walton called – George Richardson of Belford came to tea – met Miss Watson at Spindleston Hill – had a long chat with her – after I parted from her, I took a walk to meet Susan who was with the Dinnings – fine day.

Friday 21st

John Younghusband called – Miss Younghusband came to dinner – William Watson called – Miss Y and I rode into Alnwick – single horse without a beau – James rode before Susan – we drank tea with the Sandersons at the Black Swan – was introduced to Mr Liddle when I was dressing my head for the dance – he engaged me to dance the first two dances with him – I danced next with young Sanderson, then with William Watson, then with Harry Dinning – and Liddle again – and then with William Barber. Was to have danced the next two dances with Liddle but left the room before the ball gave up – we returned to the Black Swan to supper and slept there – were very much disturbed with the noise in the house – cold day.

Saturday 22nd

Alnwick – got a very uncomfortable breakfast at the Swan as all the inhabitants of the house were drunk – I called with the Dinnings at Mr Wilsons and at Major Cashells – afterwards took a walk with the Sandersons and Liddle to see the castle – this is the first time I ever was in it. Dined at Captain James with the Sanderson family where we met Mr & Mrs Howey, Miss Younghusband, Mr Liddle, Mr Nelson &c – got on horseback to return home about 5 o'clock – got a number of beaux to escort us home. James and I went round by Elwick with Margaret Younghusband – John walked halfway to Outchester to hear news of the ball – I got home at 10 o'clock – Jemima Brayson was at Outchester – a very fine warm day.

Sunday 23rd

William Barber came here to breakfast – James and I went up to the church with him – we called at Newlands – the Dinnings were so much fatigued they could not go to church. We were fortunate in going – we heard such an excellent preacher – a Mr Barns from Berwick – after dinner my uncle David and Mr Bell of Dunglass came here, and Mr Young, Mr Ostens and my cousin William came to tea – we took a walk to meet the Dinnings – as we were coming home, William and Janey Barber joined us – they came to supper – a very hot day.

Monday 24th

Mr Yellowly and Mr Whitehead the wool buyer dined here – my uncle and Mr Bell went to Link Hall and did not return until supper time – rainy day.

Tuesday 25th

Susan had a letter from Nichol saying he has been very ill of a fever – which has made me very dull indeed – my uncle and Mr Bell left us after breakfast as did my cousin Jemima Brayson. Mr North a wool buyer dined here – I have not been in such low spirits this six weeks as I am today – this day has been neither hot nor cold – had a letter from Bab D.

Wednesday 26th

Just before we sat down to tea Mr & Mrs Todd came from Berwick – we were very merry after tea – had a dance – a pleasant morning, shower in the evening – had a letter from Nichol.

Thursday 27th

Susan and I took a ride to Bambro' in the gig with Mrs Todd – Mr Todd and James accompanied us on horseback – we came home to dinner and went up to Newlands to tea where we met Dr Trotter – our Berwick frends went home after tea – this has been an unpleasant day – drizzling rain.

Friday 28th

Doctor Trotter and Harry Dinning called this morning – they sat and chatted a long time – Mr Dinning called – after I took a walk to the Low Mill, drank tea at Bradford was home before 6 o'clock – fine day.

Saturday 29th

Was scarce out of my bed today – took a long walk after tea to meet Susan who had been at Belford – pleasant day.

Sunday 30th

All the family are gone to the Meeting but me. My cousin Nichol Burrell and his wife came to dinner – this is their wedding visit – after dinner we had a walk to Spindleston Hills and after tea we walked in Bradford Dean – the evening was so pleasant that none of us could stay in the house – the Watsons are all parading about – they seem as loath as us to go into the house.

July

Monday 1st

Mr & Mrs Burrell left us after tea – Susan and I took a walk to Waren House – Joe Mole was there – he talks of going to the races at Lamberton next week – we are also speaking of it – Joe Mole escorted us home from Waren – fine day.

Tuesday 2nd

I wrote to Miss Sanderson of Swinoe – had a long chat with Mr Watson at the Burn – Dr Pringle called to see Susan's face. Miss Dinnings called after dinner for Susan and I to go to Elford to tea – we spent a very pleasant afternoon – we made James Weatherly very drunk – called at Mr Stubbs for the first time – fine day.

Wednesday 3rd

I went to Waren to see Miss Watson this morning, as I was out when she called yesterday – stopped to dinner and to tea – Miss Watson and William came to Outchester along with me – we found Mr Walton here. My Father and him were at their tea – we all took a walk to Spindleston to see old Elizabeth – wet dull day.

Thursday 4th

Quite alone – fine day.

Friday 5th

Had a letter from Miss Sanderson of Swinoe – wrote to Mr & Mrs Todd – Miss Dinnings came here to tea – Bab and I dug as many young potatoes as served our supper – we all ate off one plate – disagreeable rainy day – evening fair.

Saturday 6th

After tea I was very much astonished in going into the parlour to find young Liddle of Ewart sitting with James – his horse lost its shoe in coming past Outchester – so he was obliged to stop ere he got it fastened on – it was then too late to think of going home, so he stopped with us all night. I have been putting my dress in order for the Races – fine day.

Sunday 7th

Liddle, James and I took a ride to Belford church – we called at Newlands – a party of soldiers were marching to the north – some of them stopped in Belford today – the band played in the church – I never saw as many people in Belford church – a great many of the soldiers were obliged to stand as they could not get seats – Liddle came back to Outchester to dinner – we walked after dinner – John Younghusband and Harry Dinning called – showery day.

Monday 8th

We had some tunes upon the fiddle from Mr Liddle before he went away this morning – I went to Newlands to tea – but was there an hour before they dined – Bab and I took a walk to Belford to order a chaise for the races – the first person we met in Belford was Mr Liddle – we came home by the fields to avoid him – had a letter from Miss Watson who is in Berwick – a warm pleasant day.

Tuesday 9th

Had a deal to do today – to bake, wash, write &c and wrote to Miss Watson – Steven Thompson called after tea – I went early to bed – fine day.

Wednesday 10th

Was up at 5 o'clock – we were up at Newlands before the Dinnings were out of their beds – we got a second breakfast there and set out for Lamberton races – Miss Dinning, Susan and I in a chaise – Harry and James on horseback. We had very little sport on the race ground the day was so unfavourable – dined at Mr Todds and drank tea there – had a room full of beaux – Mr Joe Dods, Mr Tom Smith, Mr William Cook, Mr John Wilson, Mr Richard Stewart, Mr Johnstone, John Vardy and the handsome Newburn. It was nine o'clock before we could get begun to dress – I had on a green lustre gown with silver tissue sleeves – danced two dances with Joe Dods, one with Mr Todd and one with John Vardy – sat between Liddle and Vardy at supper – got a present of a pair of gloves from Joe Mole to go to the ball with – we came to Mr Todds to sleep – got a second supper there – Liddle came along with us and slept there also – wet day.

Thursday 11th

Berwick – we got down to breakfast at nine o'clock – Mr Liddle was the only beau at breakfast – we called upon the Miss Drysdales – this is the first time we were in their house – walked about the streets for about an hour – then upon the Walls. Went out to the race ground at twelve – lost three pairs of gloves – one pair to Mr Martin, a pair to Dr Trotter and a pair to Joe Dods. Had plenty of beaux when we were out but Dr Trotter was the most constant. Dined at Mr Todds – at 6 o'clock we came to Newlands to supper – Mr Jobling and Mr Winship were there. I have got a very bad cold – fine day. I have bet a pair of gloves with Grieve Smith that he will be married in the course of a week – I doubt I will lose.

Friday 12th

Quite alone – fine day.

Saturday 13th

Ditto   ditto

Sunday 14th

Was at Belford church – had the Newlands pew to myself – after dinner James and I went to Newhouses to tea, where we met Mr Wear, Mr Young, Mr Neve Trotter and John Fawcus – a fine day.

Monday 15th

Mr Young, Mr Wear and Mr N Trotter had breakfast here – Miss Bab Dinning came to tea – fine day.

Tuesday 16th

Went up to Newlands after dinner – was introduced to Mr Strickland – all walked up to West Hall. Capt'n Humble gave us a dance on Belford Crag – we danced 12 couples – we drank tea in a marquee which was erected on the hill on purpose – our music consisted of a fiddle, drum, fife and triangle – got Strickland for a beau. We danced on the hill till near 10 o'clock and then came to West Hall where thirty four of us partook of an excellent supper – we had several reels after supper. Joe Mole was very drunk – I went to Newlands all night – James and I quarrelled so I would not go home with him.

Wednesday 17th

Newlands – I am very ill of a cold and Strickland made it worse by throwing so much water upon me – we were all at the pond seeing the men take the trouts out of it – Mrs Pringle and Mrs Bromfield came to tea – I came home after tea and heard that Mr & Mrs Ross had been at Outchester to dinner and Miss Forster of Glororum came to tea – they regretted my absence very much – fine day.

Thursday 18th

Harry Dinning and Strickland called here before we were up – I soon dressed myself – wrote to Nichol – Miss Dinning bet me a pair of gloves that one of us four would have an offer before this time twelvemonth – was at a funeral today of an old woman who lived here.

Friday 19th

Just as we were sitting down to tea in popped Mr Liddle – he stopped all night – a very fine day.

Saturday 20th

The painter is here – he has painted the large parlour and is now begun the small one – the furniture is out of them both and we have not a place to sit in – Liddle helped Susan and I pull the peas for dinner – we were obliged to hull them in the arbour as we could not get into the house until 1 o'clock – Liddle went away after dinner – I have been in a very sulky temper these last two days – showery day.

Sunday 21st

James and I went to Belford church – from there to Wandylaw with the Dinnings – we came back to Belford to hear the band of music which belongs to the East Suffolk Militia – saw a very handsome officer – met a good deal of company – very pleasant day.

Monday 22nd

I was at the bathing this morning – Mrs Smith of Hay Farm and Mr Joe Watson called this morning and came back to tea accompanied by William Watson, Margaret and Miss Handyside – we danced after tea – Mr Smith civil, William Watson played a great many tunes on the fiddle – and a lame performer he is – I was in bed when the party arrived – fine day.

Tuesday 23rd

Was at Belford this morning and saw all the officers which belongs to the Westmoreland Militia – the Dinnings came down – Bab promised me a music book when I am married and Mary has promised me two pin cushion slips – my Father and James were from home, so we were very happy – showery day.

Wednesday 24th

Mr Wilson of Alnwick and Mr Kell called after tea – showery day.

Thursday 25th

I drank tea at Mr Joe Watson at Spindleston and met Miss Handyside and Miss Watson there – I walked up to Newlands to meet Susan who had been there drinking tea – they had gone to Belford – I followed them – we went with Mr Bugg to the Hall garden to get hautboys[38] and then went to the Hall to call upon Miss Holiday. Miss Brown was also there – Mr Bugg came to Newlands with us – Joe was there engaging the ladies to come to the Glendale ball – we stopped to take strawberries and cream – it was late before we got home – pleasant day.

Friday 26th

Wrote to Miss Watson – went to Newlands to tea where I met Miss Handyside and Mr Joe Watson – John Younghusband dined with us today – fine day.

Saturday 27th

James has gone to Berwick to stop a week with the Corps on permanent duty – today I was at the bathing – it rained all the time I was in the water which wet my clothes very much – came home and took ill – showery day.

Sunday 28th

Very ill – quite alone – wet day.

Monday 29th

Miss Dinnings called after tea – we walked up with them – fine day.

Tuesday 30th

Had a card from John Younghusband for to come in to the Assembly on Friday – we expect to get – I have prepared my dress – wrote to Miss Dinning – got an answer – fine day.

Wednesday 31st

My Father and Susan and I went to Link Hall to Watson Weatherly's christening where we met Mr Younghusband of Heckly Grange and his sisters, Miss Young, Mr & Mrs Trotter, Mr Redchesters, Mr & Mrs Ross &c

---

[38] Strawberries

&c – after dinner the ladies walked to Shepperton Hall[39] to see the garden. I was dressed in a sprigged muslin round dress, trimmed with chenele oak leaves and flounced with broad lace. We called at Newham Newhouses – a showery day – it was a very warm day and I had on three greatcoats with two double handkerchiefs to keep out the rain – I was almost melted with the heat. Mr Young called – I am in low spirits tonight as I don't think my Father will allow us to go to the Glendale ball. We had a great crop of strawberries this year – more than we ever had before.

---

[39] Now demolished

August

Thursday 1st

Miss Dinnings came down after tea to talk about the ball at Berwick – we are not to go. Mr Dinning called – we walked up to the turnpike with Miss Ds and met Mr Yellowly driving his housekeeper in his gig with him – Mr Watson overtook us on our return home – showery day.

Friday 2nd

I am in a very bad temper as I am disappointed for not getting to the ball – Mr Liddle and Henry Dinning came here to ask my Father – but he is quite inexorable to all their entreaties – we went to Waren House after tea – from there to Budle to meet Miss Watson and Miss Handyside – we had a walk in the garden – fine day.

Saturday 3rd

As I was walking up to Belford today who should I meet but Mr Liddle – I proceeded on my journey and he went forward to Outchester – he intended stopping all night here – Mr Dinning called – fine day.

Sunday 4th

I walked up to Belford church – went to Newlands to dinner as Mr Liddle is at Outchester – we spent the day very pleasantly and when I came home, Mr Liddle was still at Outchester – fine morning – rainy evening.

Monday 5th

I have bet with Thomas Henry Liddle this morning that if he is a Major six years from this day – I will forfeit a sword to him, value twenty guineas – if he is not, I am to have a gold watch, value twenty guineas. If he dies before that he is to leave me his gold watch enclosed in a box made in the shape of a coffin, to put me in mind of death. He took his leave of us before dinner. We were at Elwick to tea – we met Joe Mole there – William and Margaret Younghusband and Joe Mole escorted us very near home – we called at the Grange and got gooseberries and a glass of wine – very windy day.

Tuesday 6th

Mr Dinning and Mr Scott called. Susan and I took a walk to Newlands to tell Mary that Captain Bennett enquired after us at Berwick – pleasant day.

Wednesday 7th

Susan took very ill this morning. I had to go to Belford for the Doctor – he came down after dinner – William Watson came here to tea – had a letter from Miss Watson answered it – showers, fine day.

Thursday 8th

Wrote to Miss Dinning – we were drinking tea tonight with old Elizabeth – Miss Handyside, Miss Watson and William and Miss Dinning were of the party – we were all very merry – got a glass of wine after tea – weather is still changeable, showers every day.

Friday 9th

I went to Newham Newhouses after breakfast to assist Miss Young in making jelly – we dined at eleven o'clock – had a busy day but pleasant – dull weather.

Saturday 10th

Quite alone today – we made our jelly – weather the same.

Sunday 11th

Mr N Trotter and little George dined here – after tea Susan and I walked to Waren House. Mr & Mrs Crawford of Smithfield were there – we walked half way to Bambro' with them – fine day.

Monday 12th

Mr Ostens called – fine day.

Tuesday 13th

I went to Bradford to tea where I met William Humble, Mr Moffat, Mr & Mrs Maughan and Mrs Patterson – showery day.

Wednesday 14th

Miss Watson called and William & John Younghusband – we heard today that Miss Fawcus of Newham is married to a joiner she ran off with on Sunday evening – fine day.

Thursday 15th

My Father went to Scotland – I was at Newlands to dinner – Miss Dinning came down to Outchester to tea – fine day.

Friday 16th

Went to Newham to Mrs Trotters to tea – called at Newhouses – fine day.

Saturday 17th

We were at Mr Forsters of Glororum to tea – fine day.

Sunday 18th

We went to Belford church – I got myself wet to the skin – Miss Dinning was to have dined here, and then gone to Lucker to hear Mr Perigle preach – but company coming unexpectedly to Newlands prevented her – showery day.

Monday 19th

We expected company today, but it has rained incessantly since dinner – I am in a very cross temper – Mr McQueen dined here.

Tuesday 20th

As we were returning from bathing we met Mr Watson and he insisted upon us going in to breakfast, which we did – while we were there Joe Mole and his brother Patrick called. Miss Younghusband with Miss Robinson and Miss Agnus Wood came to tea – just as we were finishing our last cup, John Younghusband and Mr Ned Smith made their debut – the gents stopped to supper. After we were all gone to bed, my Father and uncles Thomas and James came from Scotland – pleasant day.

Wednesday 21st

Had a letter from Miss Dinning saying she was coming to tea – I went up to Newlands to meet her – we spent a happy evening as we were not interrupted by any male creature – a pleasant day.

Thursday 22nd

I have wrote two sheets of paper in a letter to Nichol – got a frank[40] from Mr Sitwell – my uncles and James returned from Link Hall to dinner. Mr Ostens came to tea – I was at a tea drinking at Peggy Rogersons – she has got the seventh daughter – I took a walk after dinner to Old Mill – fine day.

---

[40] Before the introduction of the Penny Post, letters could be 'franked' by M.Ps or Peers. Sitwell was MP for Berwick 1803-06.

Friday 23rd

My uncles left us after breakfast – after dinner Susan and I went to the bathing and then to Belford Fair – the Lady Hays were there – drank tea as usual at Mrs Bromfields – fine day.

Saturday 24th

Susan and I were at the bathing this morning – fine day – had a walk with Miss Watson and Ned Smith.

Sunday 25th

Susan, James and I were at Belford church – John and William Younghusband and Harry Dinning walked home with us to Outchester – after dinner we took a walk to Bradford to see Miss Nicholsons, we also saw Miss Robson and Mr Werner, and Mr Richard Robson – the latter gent escorted us to Outchester – fine day.

Monday 26th

Mr Young called this morning for Susan and I to go to Elford feast – Susan and my Father went, but I went to Newlands to see Bab as she has just returned from Newbiggin – I came home soon as I was not very well – we have begun shearing today – fine day.

Tuesday 27th

Was in bed all day – the weather is settled and now very warm.

Wednesday 28th

Mr Craster of Preston called – had a letter from Miss Dinning – fine windy day.

Thursday 29th

Quite alone – fine day.

Friday 30th

Susan was up at Newlands today – I went after tea to meet her – I met Miss Dinnings – they came down to Haverhouses with us – went back to the turnpike with them – we then met Harry and Mr Windship – they all came to the Burn with us – fine day, very hot.

Saturday 31st

I have been busy sewing chemises since Wednesday – I have finished 3 – this has been a dull day – thick fog. I wrote to Miss Ronaldson – forgot to say that William Wood of Preston was here taking leave of us on Wednesday before he joined his regiment.

September

Sunday 1st

James and I were at Warenford Meeting – after dinner we went to Newham Newhouses – Miss Young was alone as her brother has gone to Bradford to tea – he and William Weatherly came in and insisted on us staying to supper, which we did and was home at half after eight – Mr Dinning called – a showery day.

Monday 2nd

Quite alone – showery day.

Tuesday 3rd

Ditto Ditto

Wednesday 4th

Miss Bab Dinning called with Miss Cashells and Miss Seymour – Susan, James and I went to Newlands to tea – weather still soft.

Thursday 5th

I drank water to dinner – pleasant day.

Friday 6th

Had a letter from Nichol – Miss Dinnings, their brother, Miss Cashells and Miss Seymour were here to tea – Miss S is the best player on the piano I ever remember of hearing.

Saturday 7th

Had another letter from Nichol franked by Lord J Thynne – John Younghusband breakfasted here – he went to Alnwick with James and returned here to tea – the weather is still changeable.

Sunday 8th

As Mr Ross is preaching at Wooler today we all went up to Belford church – and had an excellent sermon from Mr Stopford, Lowick – Susan and I after dinner walked to Spindleston and called upon Mr Joseph Watson – Miss Watson was there – we went to Waren House and drank tea with her – we were not a little astonished to find Joe Mole on our return – he had been here to tea – he, William Watson and Margaret stopped to supper – they obtained my Father's consent to allow Susan and I to go to Berwick to see the 'Young Rocious'[41] – a warm pleasant day.

Monday 9th

Mr William Watson called this morning – Mr Walton came to dinner – I went to Newlands to tea – Miss Cashells and Miss Seymour are still there – Joe Mole drank tea at Outchester – he and James and Susan came up for me – Mole went to Newlands for supper – a very fine day.

Tuesday 10th

After dinner I walked up to Belford, drank tea with Mrs Henderson. Captain & Mrs Wallace, Miss Thompson, Mr Bowes Smith and Henderson's brother were also there. I walked home with Mr & Mrs Wallace – Bowes Smith escorted us part way – fine day.

Wednesday 11th

We set off at half after one o'clock in Mr Yellowly's gig to go to Berwick – we had not got as far as the Grange when one of the straps broke – we stopped at Mr Moles until it was mended – got into it again – called upon John Younghusband at Elwick – he out of politeness got into the gig – we did not get a few yards until down it went – the limmers[42] had broke with being too heavy a load. We were all then set on foot – got a boy to go to Belford for a chaise but they were all out – we then thought of returning home as they had not a seat[43] at Elwick, all the females having gone to Berwick. We sent to the miller's wife and borrowed one from her – James took Susan behind him and I rode single on Joe Mole's mare – I never had such a jaunt – we went to Berwick in an hour – the tea was poured out at Mr Todds but I had not time to drink it – but hasted down to Mr Pat Moles and joined a large party there to go to the play.

We stood half an hour on the staircase before the doors were opened – Master Betty performed young Norval[44] in 'The Tragedy of Douglas'. I was rather disappointed when I first heard him speak – his voice sounded harsh until accustomed a little with it – but the dying scene was beyond everything. After the play we went out, as we were afraid to stop until the entertainment,

---

[41] Stage name of Master William Betty, a child prodigy aged 13
[42] Limber boards, shafts on a horse drawn carriage
[43] Ladies' side saddle
[44] A pivotal character in the play

for the rabble coming all out at once – I went and saw Susan off – she went with Bab Dinning and Miss Cashells in the gig. Mr Tom Smith then saw me up to the Todds where I supped, drank a bottle of porter and then went to bed – rather fatigued with this days exertion – showery day.

Thursday 12th

James and I went to Smiths and bought a carpet – I then called upon most of my old acquaintances – I then went down to see the Younghusbands before they left town – Miss Watson and I called upon Redpeth and rambled about the streets – after dinner I called upon Mrs Gilchrist and was introduced to a great number of ladies and gents. Went to the play in Mr Todd's party – was very near squeezed to death in the crowd going in – I was most disagreeably situated when Mr Tom Alder offered to look out for a better seat for me, as where I was sitting we could neither hear nor see the performance – Mr Mole gave me his seat and stood himself – the first act was over when the alarm of fire was given, and some people called the Gallery was coming down. I was dreadfully frightened, two men had to hold me – some of the ladies went into hysterics, others fainted – the performance was stopped for a little while before they could get the folks persuaded that the alarm was false – two of the actresses fainted. Young Betty came on the stage and said – them people, are they all mad? Locious performed Acmet in Barbarossa – I liked him much better tonight – indeed was in raptures. This is the first time I ever knew what fear was.

We had large party to supper at Mr Todds – after I had gone up to my room, Miss Dodds of Shorewood came up to take leave of me – a very fine day.

Friday 13th

I dined at Mr Bells today – did not go out much as my clothes were so much dirtied. Mr George Bell is made a Burgess[45] today and they are to have a large party to sup – but my Father has sent for me and I will be obliged to leave Berwick. Mrs Todd is to have five smart beaux to tea – what a pity I have to go home. I called at Newlands and drank tea – heard that Miss Humble is married to Mr Watson of Unthank – got home about 8 o'clock – cannot move I am so tired – showery day.

---

[45] Freeman of the borough

Saturday 14th

Done nothing today but slept – some gentlemen called today but I do not know their names – we have been in mourning this last fortnight on account of the death of the Duke of Gloucester[46] – mourning was general in Berwick – fine day.

Sunday 15th

James and I rode over to Newham Newhouses to invite Mr Young to dinner – we afterwards went to the Meeting – Mr Herriot called – Mr Young and John Weatherly of Link Hall dined here – after dinner Mrs Henderson of Belford and Mrs Scott with James and Mary Scott, and Mr Bowes Smith – next came Mr John Ostens then Mr & Mrs Luke Scott – and while we were at tea in popped Mr Dinning and Mr Henderson and Gilbert Henderson – with our own family we were 17 in all – very fine day.

Monday 16th

Miss Dinnings called after tea – I had a letter from my cousin Burrell of Woodford – fine day.

Tuesday 17th

Mr Joe Mole called – Susan and I walked to Elwick this afternoon – Miss Agnes Wood and Miss Robinson are still there – we spent a very pleasant afternoon – made the button holes of a shirt for William – John brought us home in the gig – we called at the Grange and got pears from Joe Mole – a very stormy day, John Younghusband stopped to supper.

Wednesday 18th

Doctor Herriot called – Miss Dinnings were here to tea – Bab was in very low spirits as George Younghusband is going on the secret expedition – fine day.

Thursday 19th

Our Scotch shearers are gone this morning – our harvest was finished last night – fine day.

Friday 20th

Quite alone – fine day.

---

[46] Brother of the King, George 3rd

Saturday 21ˢᵗ

Doctor Herriot called – got a letter from Miss Ronaldson – fine day – got a new carpet tonight.

Sunday 22ⁿᵈ

I was at Belford Meeting – called at Mr Thompsons – Susan, James and I walked to Bradford to tea where we met Mr William Humble – Miss Dinnings, Harry and Mr James Blacket called here after tea – fine day.

Monday 23ʳᵈ

This being Belford Feast we all went up to Newlands after dinner – they all went to the races but me – I stopped at Newlands with Mrs Dinning – spent a very pleasant afternoon – assisted Mrs Dinning to get the tea ready – the company did not come home until it was dark – John Younghusband came first, followed by Lieutenant Sanderson, William Watson, Mr Blacket, Miss Dinnngs, and Sue escorted by our James and Joe Mole. My Father and the Nabob brought up the rear – Mrs D and I drank tea before, so I waited upon the rest as the girls were not returned from the races – Mr Renton made his debut just as the tea equipage was ready to move off – he drank tea half an hour at least – we had a dance – stopped to supper – fine day.

Tuesday 24ᵗʰ

Was in bed most part of this day – William Humble came in after tea – I got up to see him – he was very drunk – kept us laughing until 10 o'clock – fine day.

Wednesday 25ᵗʰ

Mr Walton called twice – my Father bought the houses off Easington today – the weather is still very fine.

Thursday 26ᵗʰ

Mr H Dinning sent a card – Miss Bab called this morning – I took a ride with them – met Mr Watson, called at Waren House – saw Miss Watson and Miss Handyside. My horse misbehaved sadly at the door – we next called at Mrs Humbles to see the bride – but she would not come to the door as she was not in a dress to see company. We next went to Elford and called upon Miss Mary Young – took through the fields and hunted a little while, but could not raise a hare – called at Newham Newhouses – Miss Young was kinder than anybody we have seem today – gave us bread and cheese – each of us a glass of wine – after that we called at Bradford, saw Miss Mary Ostens met Mr Richard Robson – we also called upon Mr Yellowly at Chester Hill – got pears there. Came round by Belford and home to dinner – met Miss Forster, Mr Clayton dined here. After dinner I walked up to Newlands – Mr H Dinning and I played at backgammon for about half an hour – played drafts with Mr Blacket – after tea Bab, Harry, Mr B and I went to Belford – it was late before I reached home – a very pleasant day.

Friday 27th

Miss Dinning came down this morning – Bab is making me a nankeen[47] hat – after dinner Mary and I set off for the Signal House[48] – met two gents – took a roundabout road – Captain Wallace came out to meet us – he and Mrs Wallace were so kind – we could not get away until we drank tea – we spent an uncommon pleasant afternoon. Just as we were sitting down to tea in came Mrs and Miss Watson and Miss Handyside – as we were leaving the hill met Miss Humble. Mr H Dinning had been at Outchester this afternoon, but as I from home did not stop to tea. Just as Miss Dinning went away my Father and James returned from the Fair and Mr Robert Blackadder along with them – fine day.

Saturday 28th

William Watson and John Younghusband called – Mr Dinning and his brother called before dinner and after it John Younghusband & William Watson came back to tea. Played at cards for the first time this winter – William and I against my Father and Mr Blackadder – I lost sixpence – fine day.

Sunday 29th

Mr Blackadder left us this morning – I was at Belford church – James dined and drank tea with Joe Mole – I was at Newlands – Susan was at Waren and we all returned home at the same time – called at Belford Hall with Miss Dinnings – got a letter from Mrs Fenwick Compton – fine day.

Monday 30th

Quite alone – a fine day – won eighteen pence at cards this week.

---

[47] Fashionable cotton fabric from China
[48] On Budle Hill

October

Tuesday 1st

I called at Newlands this morning upon Bab Dinning to go to Belford to buy a pelisse. I put off so much time in Belford that I was too late for my dinner – fine day.

Wednesday 2nd

Quite alone – fine day.

Thursday 3rd

Ditto   Ditto

Friday 4th

I called at Newlands this morning – Henry Dinning drank tea here – wrote to the cabinet maker – after tea Susan and I were gathering mushrooms – had a walk with Miss Watson, Miss Handyside and Mr Joseph Watson – got an invite to drink tea at Spindleston tomorrow – and another to go to the Heather House on Monday – Mr Lonsdale supped here – very fine day.

Saturday 5th

William Watson and John Younghusband called this morning for James to go to Alnwick – they also called in the afternoon just as I dressed to go to Spindleston to tea. Miss Bab Dinning came for me to go to Joe Moles – it was 4 o'clock – I went up to Newlands with Bab – we could not persuade Mary to accompany us – we then gave up all thoughts of going, but William Younghusband prevailed upon us to go – we set off on foot and arrived when the rest of the party had drunk tea and got soberly round the Whist table – tea was brought in again, but not before a full half hour had elapsed - Bab and I behaved very ill – we laughed the whole time we were in the house – after tea we all sat down to cards with Mrs Younghusband, Mr William & Miss Younghusband, Mr & Miss Robinson, Miss Wood and Miss Werge. I got happily seated between Joe and the divine William – John Younghusband was too late to get a hand at Commerce – I won the pool which was five shillings. Mrs Dinning sent horses for us – I called at Newlands on my way home – fine day.

Sunday 6th

James and I were at Warenford Meeting and after dinner we walked to Easington to Mr Scotts – we met a Mr Horsington there, he escorted us most of the way home – fine day.

Monday 7th

Mr Walton dined here – after dinner Susan and I went to the Heather House to see Miss Ostens – met Captain and Mrs Wallace there – as we were coming home met Miss Younghusband and Mr and Miss Robinson – a shower overtook us when we were at Waren, called but did not stop as all the family were from home.

Tuesday 8th

Mr Scott and Mr Horsington dined here – Miss Dinnings came to tea – we played at cards – Mr H and I went halfs and won thirteen pence at Lieu – had a very merry evening – fine day.

Wednesday 9th

I have been very ill this morning and was in bed when Susan came up and told me she saw a gentleman with my Father who had a star upon his breast. I got up in a great hurry to see our illustrious visitor – he is one of the governors for the Hospital[49] – Admiral Sir John Colpays – he was very chatty – sat a good while.

Thursday 10th

Had a busy morning marking clothes – was at Newlands to tea – Miss Dinning and I took a walk to Belford – a very pleasant day.

Friday 11th

I was busy this morning baking a cake when in came all the governors – I ran upstairs to dress but was a very short time in my room ere my Father ushered in Sir William Bellingham, who it seems wished to see the house – Mrs Forster was with him. Mr Walton and Mr Harrison came after – Mr W and I had a long chat – fine day, I wrote to Miss Ronaldson and also to Nichol – Susan wrote to him on Tuesday but Miss Dinning got a frank from Mr Sitwell so I was obliged to write again.

---

[49] Royal Greenwich Hospital – owner of Outchester

Saturday 12ᵗʰ

Mr Dinning, Mr Wales, Sir William Bellingham & Mr Collingson called this morning and sat about an hour – we are looking out for Sir John Colpays, as he promised to call today – five o'clock – he did not call. I lost sixpence at cards – stormy day.

Sunday 13ᵗʰ

William Weatherly dined here – James and I rode over to Newham Newhouses with him to tea – pleasant day.

Monday 14ᵗʰ

Susan and I called on Miss Dinnings to go to Belford – saw Joe Mole and Mr Tom Smith – returned to Newlands to tea – fine day.

Tuesday 15ᵗʰ

Mr Walton called – won sixpence at cards – the weather is beginning to break.

Wednesday 16ᵗʰ

After tea Susan and I were playing against my Father and James at Whist – I had a fine hand with five trumps in it when in came Miss Bab Dinning – James ran off with the stakes – Bab did not stop long – a disagreeable wet day.

Thursday 17ᵗʰ

Mr Black of Jedburgh came here from Wooler Fair – won sixpence at cards from him – very rainy day.

Friday 18ᵗʰ

Mr Scott and Mr Horsington dined here – James, Mr H and I were out greyhound coursing – did not get a hare – we called at Newlands saw Miss Grey there – the ladies were all preparing to go to a ball at Belford tonight. We next called at the Grange, got some apples from Joe Mole went to Easington to tea – played at cards – Mr Horsington and I against Mr Scott and James – won sixpence – we stopped to supper – very fine day.

Saturday 19ᵗʰ

Mr Horsington came here this morning – he spent the day – he did not go away until after supper – he and I were partners again at cards – won as usual – a very pleasant frosty day.

Sunday 20th

My father and I went to Link Hall this forenoon to see my aunt of Butterdean Mains who is now stopping there – we dined and came to Mr Trotters of Newham to tea – called at Newham Newhouses – William Weatherly and his brother had dined at Outchester – David was still here when we came home – fine day.

Monday 21st

My cousin David left us this morning. Bet a pair of gloves with Mr Horsington last Saturday that Joe Mole is not 30 years of age – we expect Miss Dinnings down today. I went to Newlands for them but they would not come, so stopped there. I came home early. Mr Joseph Watson was at Outchester – he won sixpence from me at cards – fine day.

Tuesday 22nd

Mr Henry Dinning called – fine day.

Wednesday 23rd

Joe Mole called this morning – I told him we expected the Dinnings to tea, so he made it convenient to come back in the afternoon – Mr Joseph Watson also drank tea. Miss Dinnings did not come – Joe Mole and I were partners at cards – won sixpence from Susan and Mr Watson – had a letter from Miss Watson – fine day.

Thursday 24th

Susan and I were busy at work this morning when in popped Bab Dinning. She told me her sister and a beau were following her – so I made my escape to adjust my dress – that done came down stairs and had the happiness to find Doctor Trotter sitting in the parlour – we went half way home with them – Miss Dinnings came back to tea – Bab baked us the best nead[50] cake that any of us had ate – it was too good – for a general sickness took place after tea – an unhappy evening we spent – pleasant morning, cold afternoon.

Friday 25th

Miss Young, Mrs Thomas Weatherly and Mrs William Weatherly came here to dinner. My aunt and cousin went away before tea – they took Susan along

---

[50] A cake for a celebration

with them. Miss Young stopped and had a hand at cards – James and I won eighteen pence from my Father and her – cold day

Saturday 26th

I was at the Meeting this afternoon and came to Bradford to tea – was soon home – I durst not stop late being on foot – this day has been very dull and showery – had a letter from Miss Ronaldson and a pale blue sarsanet gown from Edinburgh – it is very handsome and fits delightfully.

Sunday 27th

This is the Sacrament day at Warenford Meeting – all our family were of course there – Mr Atkin of Etal assisted Mr Ross – had an excellent sermon from him this afternoon – dined as usual with the priest. Mr John Younghusband was at Outchester when we came home – we expected Mr William Barber of Boomer today – but he has not come – fine day but cold.

Monday 28th

I was at Warenford Meeting this morning again to hear Mr Atkin preach and was very much edified by his sermon – went to Link Hall to dinner and accompanied my cousins to Shepperton Hall to tea – spent a most delightful afternoon – Mrs Kay was very kind – her brother and sister were there – we danced after tea – I am quite in love with little Albert Kay – he is so polite. Miss Kay played on the piano and sang – she is a very indifferent singer – but I daresay she will improve – we were laden home with flowers. I went to Link Hall for my horse and got home about nine o'clock – had my blue gown on for the first time – wrote to Miss Dinning – had a letter from Barbara – showery day. Mr Atkin and Doctor Cockayne had been at Outchester to tea – the Doctor had gone before I got home, but Mr Atkin was still here and stopped all night.

Tuesday 29th

Mr Atkin left us immediately after breakfast. I went to Newlands after dinner – Bab and I walked to Belford – called upon Mrs Henderson and Mrs Scott – returned to Mr Dinnings to tea – Mr Redchester was there. Spent a very pleasant evening – but was rather vexed when I heard that Mrs Watson and Miss Redpeth had been at Outchester. Mr Wild was at Belford – fine day.

Wednesday 30th

Just as I was putting the turkeys to rest, Miss Dinnings and Doctor Trotter drove up to the door – they were a very few minutes in the house ere we began to play at cards. Bab and I played against the Doctor and my Father – we were rather many for them. James and the Doctor then tried us for a shilling a game – we neither lost nor won – Miss Dinning was very prim as Trotter is one of her beaux – fine day.

Thursday 31st

Mr Watson called to see me this morning as he had something of great importance to communicate – it was about Bab Dinning's beau, Mr Wild – I called upon Miss Watson to go to the Friars to see Miss Redpeth. Miss W, Miss Redpeth and I went to the castle to see Miss Maughan – we stopped about an hour there – we played at Commerce – I lost half a crown – Watson of Unthank was there – Harry Dinning called here – fine day.

November

Friday 1st

John Younghusband called for James and I to come to Elwick to tea – I could not fix, as Jim was out hunting – he did not come home until after five o'clock – though it was late, rather than disappoint John we set off for Elwick to tea – Harry Dinning was there – Miss Wood, Miss Carr, Miss Robinson. We were much astonished to hear that is was their Kirn tonight, as John did not say a word about it in the morning. H Dinning would not stop to get a dance - we went out into the Granary after supper and stopped for about an hour – was highly gratified with seeing the girls – they were dressed so ridiculously. It was after one o'clock before we went to bed – Miss Carr and I slept together – we talked until three o'clock. William Younghusband and I won sixpence from Miss Wood and James – fine day.

Saturday 2nd

Elwick – William Watson called – was busy this morning running the heels of William Younghusband's stockings – after that took a walk to meet Mrs Oswald Younghusband who came up to dinner – her son and daughter were with her – after dinner Doctor Herriot came in – I came home to tea – wrote Miss Ronaldson this week and Bab Dinning – got very little work done as I have visited so much – fine frosty day.

Sunday 3rd

James and I were at Warenford Meeting – came out at half preaching to go to hear Lord Grayson preach at Rock – we had just got as far as the gate at Link Hall when we saw Susan returning from church – I was very much disappointed – we dined at Link Hall – called at Charlton and got a seat to bring Susan home – we came to Newlands to tea – old Mr Trotter of Dunse was there – had a huge deal of news as we had not seen the Miss Dinnings for four days – a very pleasant day but cold.

Monday 4th

After dinner I took a walk to Bradford – spent the afternoon with the Miss Ostens but came home to tea – Mr William Blackadder was here when I returned – he and I were partners at cards, lost sixpence – he stopped all night – frosty day.

Tuesday 5th

William went away after breakfast – James is gone into Berwick with the Glendale on permanent duty – the rest are to go tomorrow, but he has gone before to get lodgings – we are expecting a ball on Friday – Blackadder came back to dinner – we also had Mr & Mrs Ross – they went home after tea but Mr Blackadder stopped all night.

Wednesday 6th

Susan and I were paying the wedding visit to Mr Thompson – the Burge[51] priest – spent a very pleasant evening – the Dinnings were at Belford – we walked so far on the road home with them and chatted about the ball – fine day.

Thursday 7th

When the girl came to tell me to get up this morning, she gave me a letter into my bed – it was from Miss Watson for me to go down to fix how we were to go to Berwick – after breakfast the post boy came in with a letter from James saying the dance was to be tonight – I had scarce got the letter read when a servant from Elwick arrived with an express from Miss Wood – I wrote to Newlands and then went down to Waren House – I wrote from there to Miss Wood – Miss Watson and I fixed to go to Berwick in a chaise – we next thought of preparing our dresses – I had on a blue sarsanet and a net hair band – after dinner the chaise came for us – it was the two o'clock – called for Miss Watson.

When we went to Waren, Mr Bell and Mr Nesbit were there – Budle business was just finally settled, so got a glass of wine to drink good luck to it – we next called at Elwick. I almost made Margaret and Susan stupid, I talked so much until William Blackadder came up, he rode some miles along side of the chaise – got in to Berwick about five o'clock.

Bab Dinning met us – we drove to Mr Bells – had a walk before tea – was soon dressed, went over to Mrs Walkers and officiated as hairdresser to Miss Watson – went into the ballroom in Mrs Adam Thompson's party. Danced the first two country dances with George Bell – next with Tom Dodds, then with Richard Steward – sat between John Vardy and Tom Dodds at supper – got very intimate with Mr Dunn of Buckton – had a most

---

[51] Burgher, a minister of the Secession church

excellent dance – got home escorted by Richard Steward and George Bell at 5 o'clock – George gave us a strong brandy – before we got to bed another hour had elapsed – so it was six o'clock – Mrs Grieve Smith was a bride at this ball – fine fine fine day.

Friday 8th

Mr Bells Berwick – got up at eight o'clock and went to Mr Todds for breakfast where I met William Smith and Mr Barber, Doddington. Miss Dinnings, Miss Watson with Susan came up to Mr Todds to see the troop pass – the Berwickshire came first, the Glendale next and the North Durham brought up the rear. While we were looking out at the window who should we recognise but Bab Dinning's beau, Mr Wild – Susan and Bab went out and he joined them. Miss Dinning, Miss Watson and I went out to make morning calls – first we went to see Mrs Adam Thompson, and then called upon Miss Redpeth, Miss Werge, Mrs Alen Shaw, Mrs Kennedy – took a walk upon the walls – met Susan and Bab with Wild – we did not join them but came down and called upon Mrs Dunlop – Doctor Trotter joined us – we then called upon Mrs Doctor Stevenson – I was then left alone. I called upon Mrs Gilchrist – Mrs Cully and Mrs Robinson were there. Miss Sarah Todd then went out with me to call upon Mrs John Bell and Miss Drysdales. We then went down to meet with the rest of our party, but they were not come, so I went and called upon Mrs Rankin – she gave me a full account of my cousin George's wedding.

I then went and dressed for dinner – went upon the bridge to see a ship launched and was joined by all the beaux of our acquaintance – got back to dinner at 4 o'clock – Miss Dag, Mr Air, Mr John Logan, Mr George Brown, Mr John Vardy, James, Susan and I dined at Mr Bells – Miss Watson came over after dinner. We were dancing after tea and in high spirits when we thought of going to the play – set off at eight o'clock to the theatre got comfortably seated between George Brown and Tom Smith.

The play was bespoke by Captain Bennett which was 'Diamond Cut Diamond'[52]. It was just over when we heard a great noise in the street, and shortly after a flag of victory[53] was brought into the theatre, with the joyful news that nineteen sail of the line were taken. But a damp was soon thrown

---

[52] Also known as 'Venetian Revels', a Covent Garden production
[53] The battle of Trafalgar fought on 21st October

over the general joy when we heard that the brave Admiral Nelson had fallen in the action – nothing was heard for some minutes for the shouts of the people – Sir Carnaby Haggerston began to harangue the nobility, but the wine had been too potent at dinner for anyone to be edified by his bright speeches. Captain Bennett got the newspaper in and read it 'pro bonna publico' – when he came to the place which announced the death of Lord Nelson, he spoke with such feeling that it brought a starting tear into every eye present. Tom Smith and I were saying how prettily he read &c &c when we were told he was just at our back and overheard every word. 'Rule Britannia' was sung by the players and joined in chorus by everybody that had a voice either to roar or sing.

John Vardy, Tom Smith and Colonel Brown came down with us to Mr Bells to supper. We sat up until morning as the gents would not let us go away for all the news was canvassed over and over again – the memory of Lord Nelson was drunk after supper. This has been one of the busiest days I have had this some time – got to bed a little after one, but was very much disturbed by Harry Dinning and John Younghusband calling oyez – very fine day.

Saturday 9th

Mr Bells Berwick – got up at nine, went to Mr Todds to breakfast, where I met Miss Watson, Miss Dinnings, John Vardy, Tom Smith, George Brown, Tom Dodds &c &c. After that went out for a walk with William Watson, Margaret and Joe Mole – called at Mrs Walkers – were through half the shops in Berwick trying to get a feather for Joe Mole – got a letter from my Father saying he could not send horses in for us – a Mr Smith of Stockton offered to take a chaise for us. Susan made a conquest of him at the ball – being a stranger, we could not with propriety accept his polite offer. Went to a china shop to choose a set of china, but so many beaux put me quite stupid – however with the help of the Dinnings made a choice of a set with landscapes drawn on them. I then went down the street with Tom Smith who bought Miss Watson and I each a smart whip – next went to get a dozen of knives and forks and a pair of patent snuffers – was as stupid there – Susan went home with the Miss Dinnings.

John Younghusband, Margaret Watson and I paraded the streets for two or three hours – called upon Redpeths – met Mrs Grieve Smith there – came down to Mr Todds where I stopped to dinner. Soon after Mr John Segan, Mr

John Todd came in but they did not stop long – but William Smith, Tom Dodds, George Bell brought Mr Smith. I had to bear with patience some very severe rubs for saying I was going home with John Younghusband in the gig. Miss Watson came down to see me or rather to see the beaux that were at Mr Todds. John came for me – as near as I can recollect, the gentlemen who came to see me into the gig were as follows – Tom Dodds, Tom Smith, Dick Steward, Mr Todd, Johnston,(Stockton Mr Smith), William Smith, George Bell, Robert Gilchrist, John Todd and John Logan.

I came to Elwick about 7 o'clock and found Miss Wood and William Younghusband sitting very quietly reading the papers – stopped at Elwick all night – misty day.

Sunday 10th

Elwick – William and John went away from us after breakfast – Miss Carr called and Doctor Cockayne – I took the foot of the table at dinner – gave toasts after – the King – memory of Lord Nelson – Elwick family – Ross family and good news from Learmouth. Miss Wood and Miss Robinson came home with me to tea – Mr William and John came to supper – wrote to John and Mrs Todd – cold day.

Monday 11th

After breakfast I went up to Newlands – saw the Dinnings – Bab escorted me down part of the way – had a pleasant chat – Mr Walton called here after tea – I had him for a partner at cards and lost a shilling – chilly cold day.

Tuesday 12th

Mr Dinning called – wrote to Nichol – about eight o'clock I was rather astonished when I heard rap and saw Mr Smith and Mr Elstob of Stockton enter – they stopped to supper – fine day.

Wednesday 13th

Quite alone – fine day.

Thursday 14th

Mr Thompson of Scremerston called with Harry Dinning – we were at dinner but they would not partake – in a few minutes afterwards in popped Mr Smith – I was engaged to go to Newlands and although we had a beau it did not prevent me. Sandy Thompson was still there – Mary smiled once upon him – which fluttered the poor fellow, he could not compose himself again. Bab and I took a ride to Belford to read the paper – it was quite dark but quite pleasant – got home very soon which was uncommon, but it was on Mr Smith's account he was still here and if I am not mistaken, may take up his abode for a few days – fine day.

Friday 15th

Mr Dinning called with Mr Johnston of Berwick – Johnston stopped to dinner and we all went to Newlands to tea, from there to Belford to see and hear Miss Le Sugg the infant Billington[54] and Rocius. In the first place the fellow, her father, imposed upon all the inhabitants by making us pay a shilling more than was marked on the bill – it rather put the company into a sulky mood – Harry Dinning and I were both upon one chair – we were indifferently entertained – got brandy punch and negus after. I offered Johnston a new hat if he could persuade Colonel Brown to take me 'for better for worse' we came home to supper and were very happy for an hour or two after – fine day.

Saturday 16th

Johnson left Outchester after breakfast – Christopher Smith junior Esq. bet me a dozen pairs of gloves I will be married before or at the expiration of two years of this day and date hereof. I held the bet of course, as I will win however it is. John Younghusband called as did Mr Dinning – Mr D kindly invited Mr Smith to his house to dinner – they both stopped here – Mr Dinning went away after dinner and Mr Smith promised to follow him in ten minutes, which he did, but was not long in returning again for he lost the road. Susan and I took compassion on the youth and walked up to Newlands with him. I very near blushed when I went in as it was the third time I have been there this week. Harry and I played at cards and won eighteen pence from Mary and Mr Smith – we had a merry dance – stopped to supper. I went upstairs with Barbara while the girl was laying the cloth for supper – but what a shock I did get when Bab informed me that Mr Smith had offered to Susan and they were engaged for life – to a man she has only been acquainted with for a week – fine day.

---

[54] Child prodigy aged 7

November 1805

Sunday 17th

Were all at Belford church. Miss Dinnings, Miss Wilson and Nichol Burrell came to tea. Spent a most uncomfortable afternoon as all the gents were rather groggy – the ladies went away soon – fine day.

Monday 18th

I took a walk to Belford this morning to get each of us a dark blue greatcoat. Miss Wilson and Bab Dinning were there – came home to dinner and after that we took a walk to Spindleston Hills – we were agreeably surprised to see a smart beau coming from Outchester to join us – it happened to be Mr Johnston – he stopped to tea – he and I played at Whist against my Father and James, a shilling a rubber – we won of course as Johnston is the best partner I ever had, engaged to him the first Whist table we met at – he went away and I got James for a partner against Smith and Susan – they were so stupid we got the rubber very easy – fine day.

Tuesday 19th

After dinner James and I rode up to Newlands to call on the Dinnings to go to Elwick – Miss Wilson came with them – Susan and Mr Smith came the other road. Mr Pratt and Doctor Herriot were also at Elwick – played at Speculation[55] *– I won eighteen pence. William Younghusband never spoke to any of us, but was in the sulks the whole evening – we came round by Belford for company to the Dinnings – we were thirteen in company at Elwick – they told us something would happen – which was verified as Susan fell off. Mr Smith was so foolish as to get off the horse before her, and it kicked her off at the stable door. I had a long tête a tête with Smith in the little parlour last night about his engagement with Susan – he and I quarrelled – however we are better friends tonight, as he will insist on me taking his gold watch for to keep as for his sake – however I refused it. Nichol Burrell and my Father had supped before we got home – rainy day.*

Wednesday 20th

Was quite transported this morning when I got a letter with the Duns post mark on it, as I thought it was an invite to a wedding, but is was only a card from the directors of the Duns ball. My cousin Burrell and Mr Smith left us after dinner – the latter gent was very civil – poor fellow he was very much affected when he took leave of us – a very dull day.

---

[55] Popular card game frequently mentioned by Jane Austen

131

Thursday 21st

I was sitting very dull this afternoon (Doctor Cogham and Mr Warnum called) when I received a note from Bab Dinning for me to come up to Newlands behind their servant – they were all very dull about Miss Cashells who had called there this morning on her return from Edinbro' – poor thing she is given up by the doctors – we spent a pleasant evening – fine day.

Friday 22nd

Newlands – took a walk to Belford this morning – Mary sported her new velvet pelisse – it rained as we were returning home & I was under the necessity to give her my cloth pelisse on above hers. Bab went to Outchester after dinner to see Susan – she was busy at work when she returned. She astonished me very much when she told me this was my cousin Grace Hood's wedding day[56] & that a servant had come to Outchester with a card for us to go to Bowshiel to dinner – it was a great disappointment to me, I have so long spoken of going to Berwickshire – showery day.

Saturday 23rd

Newlands – was very ill this morning, could not come downstairs until eleven o'clock – came home after dinner and went to bed – got a letter from Nichol franked by Lord Thynne – pleasant day but cold.

Sunday 24th

My Father and Susan have gone to the Meeting – James and I went over this morning to Spindleston and had a chat with Mr Joe Watson – been rather poorly today – weather fine.

Monday 25th

Wrote to Mrs Hood, Chalkie Law. Mr Yellowly was here to dinner. Mrs Hall came after – we were under the disagreeable necessity of having her as we were already engaged to drink tea at Bambro' castle with Miss Maughan, and to meet the Dinnings there – we got to the castle before the company rose from dinner – Mr Bowlt, Mr Robinson of Tuggal, Mr Charles and Mr Lewis Perigal were at Maughans. We played at cards after tea. I neither lost nor won, but Susan lost four shillings as Mr Maughan kept teasing her about Mr Smith – the gentlemen were very civil to Bab Dinning & when we came

---

[56] Grace Hood of Bowshiel married Thomas Hood of Chalkie Law

away Mr Bowlt threw Mr Lewis Perigal into the cart – the Dinnings came so far home with us in the cart – very fine day.

Tuesday 26th

I was busy this afternoon pickling beetroot when in popped the Miss Dinnings – we spent a pleasant night as my Father and James were engaged. Mary and Susan penned a millimass to Doctor Turnbull – fine day.

Wednesday 27th

I have been nineteen times in a passion today – we expected a party to dinner at 2 o'clock – then James said three – Joe Mole came at 2 but none of the others came until four. Miss Wood and Miss Robinson with John Younghusband – Harry Dinning came next and as we were at dinner, in came William Younghusband – he and John had been out with Bailies hounds – we got dinner at candle light – spent rather a dull day – was at high words with William Younghusband – they all stopped to supper but Dinning. I hear today that Mrs Compton has got a son on Sunday last – have won a pair of gloves by it – very fine day.

Thursday 28th

James and my Father were at a race today on Ross sands – it was a match between Colonel Hunter and Alder of Horncliff – they came home in great spirits. Mr Horsington came here to dinner with them – played cards after tea – Mr H and I against my Father and Susan – had four rubbers – neither lost nor won – the weather is remarkable fine.

Friday 29th

Mr Horsington and Joe Mole were here to breakfast – they went to hunt at Ellingham wood with the Bailies hounds – they returned home in a very bad humour as Mr Beaug of Hoppen had spoiled all the sport by planting the ground before they arrived. Mr Dinning and Harry called, Mr Graham their landlord was with them. Mr Walton called this morning and sang over his songs which he has composed – after we had drunk tea, Mr & Mrs Scott & James came – we were busy at cards as usual and so intent upon the game, I could not rise to receive them – Susan got them their tea and we sat down to a round game. Lieutenant Horsington and I went halfs – won three shillings between us – they stopped to supper. Susan saves me a great deal of trouble now as she gets the supper ready and goes far more about the house than she used to do – fine day.

Saturday 30th

Susan got a letter from Mr Smith this morning. I wrote to Smith the tailor about a habit – Mr Horsington called – went to Newlands to tea - was at Belford – fine day, got terribly wet coming home – it rained.

December

Sunday 1st

My father would not allow me to go to the Meeting it was such a stormy day – but James and I rode over to Newham Newhouses to tea – Mr Ostens was there – Mr Horsington came to tea.

Monday 2nd

Quite alone – fine day.

Tuesday 3rd

……….frosty.

Wednesday 4th

Bab Dinning called this morning & while she was here a parcel arrived from Mr Smith containing a gold allegrech[57] bandeau, cornelian brooch and ear rings – a gold chain and locket – accompanied by a very polite card – the same to Susan – very fine day.

Thursday 5th

Went to Belford church as this is a thanksgiving day on account of the late victory – we called at Newlands, both going and coming from church – Bab Dinning came home with us & Doctor Cockayne came to dinner – got cold meat as my Father had dined before we got home. Mr Watson came to tea and Mr Yellowly – Margaret, Susan and Bab left me after tea & I was under the disagreeable necessity to sit and play at cards with the old folks – Mr Yellowly and I against my Father and James – we won the first rubber and lost the second – Miss B.D stopped all night – fine day.

Friday 6th

We were busy this morning making a black velvet pelisse – did not get it finished as we wished to accompany Bab home as we had not seen Mary since yesterday morning – fine day.

Saturday 7th

Wrote to Nichol and sent him a box full of songs and catechisms – I copied four off last night for him – fine day.

---

[57] Probably 'a la grecque' – in the Greek style

Sunday 8th

I was at Warenford today – Mr & Miss Young of Brunton were in our pew – Susan and I were at Spindleston – after dinner we called upon Mr Joseph Watson – cold day.

Monday 9th

We were all at Newham Newhouses today, this being their feast – the Link Hall family and Mr Ostens were also there – I lost 4 shillings at cards – cold frosty day.

Tuesday 10th

Quite alone – frosty day.

Wednesday 11th

I walked up to Belford this afternoon to the weavers. Bab Dinning was also there – we called upon Mrs Henderson and tea with Mrs Scott – after tea we went up to Mrs Bromfields - Bab was writing to Miss Wilson when in jumped George Younghusband – nothing could exceed our astonishment as we never heard of him being in the country – he and Bab escorted me part of the way home – fine day, hard frost.

Thursday 12th

Susan is in a terrible dilemma – as my Father has to see Mr Smith's letter. Miss Dinnings came down to tea – their brother and George Younghusband soon followed – Bab is perfectly stupid. She ordered the girl to place the candles on a table at the door to let them see to play at cards – I was Harry's partner & lost two shillings – I came to the other table and soon won my money back – George & I against Bab and my Father – he was not so much in love as his partner and was often heard to say 'Miss Barbara you are taking all my tricks' – poor girl, her confusion never let her see a card that was played. I think George is still very fond of her – very frosty day, stormy.

Friday 13th

This day is so stormy it is hardly possible to stir out of the house……..

Saturday 14th

Harry Dinning called this morning – still very stormy.

Sunday 15th

I was at the Meeting at Warenford today – we were all sitting very dull after dinner when in popped Mr Dinning – he petitioned my Father to allow me to go up to Newlands all night – I went – so we did not get to sleep until Monday morning – Bab was so ill with the heartburn from eating too freely at supper – frosty, stormy.

Monday 16th

Newlands – got up at 10 o'clock – we went to Belford and from there to West Hall, met William Humble and Mr John Watson there - had a long chat with Mrs Humble - it was a charming frosty morning, but dirty walking. We called at Mrs Cooks and at Mrs Scotts, Mrs Hill &c &c. I did not leave Newlands until after tea – pleasant frosty day.

Tuesday 17th

George Younghusband called – I wrote to Bab Dinning – got an answer.

Wednesday 18th

Very pleasant day.

Thursday 19th

Got a letter from my cousin Hood of Chalkie Law – the first I have received from her since she was married – wrote a card to Miss Drysdale – this is the first day the snow has gone off the ground – remarkable fine day.

Friday 20th

William Barber was married to Miss Sarah Anderson last Tuesday – stormy day.

Saturday 21st

Cold day.

Sunday 22nd

While we were sitting at dinner a post chaise drove to the door & in a few seconds Mr Smith was announced. Susan was agreeably surprised – it had the contrary effect upon me. The weather is like to settle – Mr S looks much better than when we first saw him at Berwick.

Monday 23rd

Miss Dinnings, their brother, George and John Younghusband dined here. Barbara and George carried on a great flirtation. She and Susan were very conceited – so much so that they would not sit in the same room as their beaux, but went upstairs during most part of the evening. John Younghusband and Mr Smith got themselves beastly drunk – the party stopped to supper – unpleasant day.

Tuesday 24th

Called at Newlands this morning – Bab Dinning went to Belford along with us – from there we went to West Hall – a great number of farmers were in town today – I counted twenty four - a rare sight – George and John Younghusband joined us – we called at Captain Cooks – fine frosty day.

Wednesday 25th

We were all at Belford church – heard Mr Stopford preach – sat in the Younghusband's pew. John, George and James all behaved very ill – laughed immoderately – this being Xmas day we got goose pie in McDonalds[58] – we were a large party – Younghusbands, Dinnings, Miss Wood, young Selby of Twizel, Mr Smith &c &c – a very fine day.

Thursday 26th

We were at Newlands to dinner where we met Captain and Mrs Humble, the Younghusbands, Joe Mole. I spent a charming day though I was sadly neglected – Mr Smith looked everything to Susan – George paid marked attention to Barbara as usual – Joe Mole was very sweet upon Mary & I never got a civil thing said to me except from Captain Humble or Mrs Dinning. Mr Smith treat us with a chaise to & from Newlands – it was one o'clock before we got home – James was mildly drunk – Mr Smith, stupidly so.....pleasant morning, stormy afternoon.

Friday 27th

We have done nothing today but walked about the fields with Mr Smith – cold day.

---

[58] The Blue Bell

Saturday 28th

Mr Smith, Susan and I walked to Waren House – sat there about an hour and then took a ramble about the sea side – William and Margaret walked a while along with us – it rained before we could reach home – took shelter below a crag at Spindleston Hills – Miss Dinning came down here to tea – Mary & I went upstairs to have a little conversation – we were almost suffocated with smoke. Mr Smith came up to see what we were after – he could not perceive us for some little time – until he heard the sound of our tongues at the fireside – we had on greatcoats for the windows were thrown open to let in air – cold day.

Sunday 29th

James and I were at the Meeting & when we came home we found Mr Johnston of Berwick & James Wilson here – they were both very chatty and agreeable – they left us after dinner – James and Smith went to Newlands to tea & Susan and I took a walk over to Spindleston to see Mr Joseph Watson – very pleasant day.

Monday 30th

Was awoke this morning by Susan saying that Mr Smith was on the point of death. I had only left him about an hour before – we were all very much alarmed, as he said himself he had only a few moments to live – he made his Will & left Susan six hundred pounds & me his gold watch – James his chaise and a pair of new boots & the Dinnings and I were each to have mourning rings – he was quite delirious for four hours – James and I were obliged to hold him in bed – he recovered a little before dinner but soon took ill again. Susan went to bed as she had not visited her pillow since Saturday night. Mr Anthony Barber came to tea & James and my Father were under the necessity of drinking tea with his Lordship & I was left with Mr Smith in a high fever – he was very cross when he was able to speak. I had to read sermons this whole day – a sorry nurse I make, as patience is not in my catalogue of virtues. The doctor made his debut after supper & I was then relieved of my charge. Mr Trotter and Mr Lonsdale called – the weather is wet and stormy.

Tuesday 31st

Mr Smith still continues very poorly – he got downstairs to see the doctor who called this morning – am very much afraid he is subject to these fits as he tells me he was affected in the same manner some years ago – he was able to play a rubber at cards – but after he went up to his room again, had a relapse – I paid him unremitting attention – for which he seemed very grateful – fine day.

Then follows two lines crossed out; she perhaps realised that it was 1st January.

This is a page from the diary; the occasion is not specified.

Head of the Table at Supper
Blancmange Eggs   Cockles   Sliced Ham
Butter   Apple Jelly   Lobster
Beetroot   Preserved Oranges   Whipped Cream
Celery   Preserved Pears
Carrots   Hedgehog   Potatoes
Brawn   Roasted Chickens   Cranberry Open Tart
Ornamented with Boxwood

The correct term for Blancmange Eggs is 'Hen's Nest' – egg shells pierced, drained, filled with blancmange like mixture, allowed to set, peeled and then set on a bed of calves jelly. Hedgehog is also a blancmange type confection, allowed to set in a bowl or mould, turned out and spiked with strips of blanched almonds in the manner of a hedgehog.

Expenses for the year 1805

Eleanor's original spelling has been retained in this section and the Scriptiana.

	£	s	d
Jan			
A comb		10	0
Gold fastener for beads		1	0
Lost bet of pr of gloves which cost		3	0
A ruby velvet bonnet	1	1	0
A box of lip salve			8
A shawl		12	0
A brooch		4	6
Spirit of roses		5	0
Making a white morning gown		2	0
Feb			
Pr of pea green glove leather shoes		7	0
Bottle of liquid blue		1	0
Qtr yard of muslin		1	0
A dark morning gown		10	6
A brown calico petticoat		5	4
Making the morning gown		2	0
Making a cloth peleese		2	6

	£	s	d
Mar			
Pr of black morrocha shoes		6	0
To soaling a pair		3	0
Purple ribbon		2	2
Pink ribbon			6
Silk thread			6
Paste board			3
Silk thread			4
Silk thread		1	0
5 yds flannel at 2/2 per yard		10	10
Glass buttons		5	0
Silk cord		2	0
Spy glass		6	0
Postage at sundry times		5	0
Pair of gaiters		4	0
Cambrick muslin petticoat		14	3
Wine muslin for frills		4	0
Apr			
Cambrick for Habit shirts		12	0
For sundry expenses		5	0
A pair of bibles		13	0
Green ribbon		6	0
White ribbon			7

	£	s	d
Black ribbon		6	0
Cottin cambrick muslin gown	1	16	0
Lining		1	11
Making		2	0
Tape and brown ribbons		1	0
Expences at Belford ball		4	0
Pair of short gloves		1	10
Pair of long gloves		3	8

May

	£	s	d
A cambrick muslin spencer		10	6
A straw bonnet	1	18	0
Ribbons		4	0
Making up and dying an old gown		4	0
A comb		3	6
Straw coloured ribband		3	0
Brown coloured ribband		1	3
A cheked muslin kerchief		2	0
Bloom muslin		3	0
Wine muslin		1	0

Jun

	£	s	d
Pair of glove leather shoes		6	0
Pair of morocco glove leather shoes		6	3
Altering a gown		1	7

Expenses

	£	s	d
For brown chineele		1	6
A Dimity bonnet		6	6
Pair of white gloves		1	6
Thimble		1	6
Lavender water			6
Pink ribbon			3
Jul			
A blue cotton gown	1	1	3
Green ribbon		1	4
Leno muslin		1	6
Aug			
Making and altering gowns		6	0
Lavender water		1	6
Pair of black morocco shoes		6	6
Pr of Habit gloves		2	0
2 pr white cotton stockings		9	6
Sep			
A white leno half shawl		6	0
Black silk half kerchief		2	4
Qtr yard of cambrick muslin		1	0
Pair of white silk stockings		12	6
A nankeen hat		4	6

	£	s	d
Oct			
Flesh coloured ribbon		4	6
Nankeen peleese	1	3	6
Shoes		7	6
1 yd cambric		7	0
For making the pelisse		4	0
For strings to it			8
A blue sarsenet gown	2	9	6
Lining and pad		3	6
Making		6	6
Cord and buttons		7	6
Cotton		4	6
Blue ribbon			8
Altering a gown		1	6
Nov			
White kid shoes		6	0
White kid gloves		3	9
Mending trinkets		3	0
Dying stockings		2	0
Hair band		5	0
Black ribbon		1	0
Dec			
Muslin for long sleeves		2	0

	£	s	d
A great coat	*2*	*12*	*0*
A black velvet peleese	*4*	*2*	*0*
Altering gowns, mantua maker		*3*	*0*
Gloves cleaning 6 prs		*3*	*0*
Leno Habit shirt		*4*	*6*
Black shoes		*7*	*6*
Leno Habit shirt		*4*	*6*
Claret Habit	*4*	*15*	*0*
Black boarder	*1*	*5*	*0*
2 pairs stocking at 6/6 each		*13*	*0*
Total	*42*	*11*	*2*

Some extra expenses I have omitted to mention – I think £50 will cover the whole

Extracts from Eleanor Weatherly's Scriptiana

A Recipe how to make a modern Romance

To procure an old court calendar and take out a few Lords and Dowagers; there is no occasion to pick them, but must be careful they are sufficiently acid. Stew them for some time in an old castle, stirring them up at times with a giddy young creature that is wiser than them all; set them on again adding an Ensign of the Guards, a little spice of a city grocer, and a lawyer or two, but keep them from boiling over by a dash now and again of sentiment or morality. If they are not seasoned enough, must add a few city cousins with airs and graces; then take out the Ensign and giddy girl and lay them on a dish by themselves; if the others are too hot, set them by 'till they cool.

Literary and Fashionable Magazine 1808

To cure a Nervous Lady

Take of birch rods a handful.

Directions – To be applied to the small of the back every third hour and a sufficient number of warm words and oaths to be given at the same time. The patient to be confined to a dark room two hours every day. Repeat these operations till she be cured. A very strong bitter draught, (without spirit) to be given till she declares that she is better.

Jan 1817

Punch Exquisite

Take twenty bottles of sparkling Champagne, add six bottles of the finest Jamaican Rum, seven pounds of double refined sugar clarified, nine wine glasses of Lime Juice, six tablespoons Lemon Juice, three wine glasses of Arrack and by way of colouring thrown in two bottles of real Cognac. As soon as the above is properly mixed and filtered through blotting paper, a most Elegant and Brilliant beverage is produced, ready for immediate use.

Recipe for a Fashionable Rout

Take all the Gentlemen and Ladies you can get, place them in a room with a slow fire, stir them well, have ready a pianoforte, a harp, a handful of Books or Prints, put them in from time to time when the mixture begins to settle sweeten with politeness or wit (if you have it) if not, flattery will do as well and is very cheap. When all have stewed together for two or three hours, put in one or two turkeys, some tongue, sliced beef or ham, tarts, cakes and sweetmeats and some bottles of wine, the more you put the better and the more substantial your Rout will be.

NB- Fill your room quite full and let the sum run off itself.

English Champaigne

Boil in six gallons of water, eighteen lbs of loaf sugar for half an hour carefully taking off the scum as it rises.- and pour it boiling hot over two gallons of fine large white currants, picked from the stalks but not bruised. In the liquor becoming near the temperature of new milk, ferment it with some good ale yeast, and after suffering it to work two days, strain it through a flannel bag into a barrel which it completely fills, with half an ounce of isinglass – on its ceasing to ferment immediately bottle it off and put in each bottle a lump of double refined sugar.

We add a bottle of brandy to each ten gallons of the wine and allow it to stand till winter.

Gooseberries not fully ripe may be used in the same manner, neither of which should be bottled in windy weather.

Handy Hints

A piece of red hot chain a quarter of a yard long is a good substitute for coals in a warming pan.

Salt of lemons to wash lace or muslin that is stained

Rice flour makes the best cement for joining paper

Blotting paper wetted and made firm will take ink out of mahogany

Lemon Spunge

Dissolve one ounce or rather less of Isinglass in half a pint of water, quarter of a pound of sugar and the rind of one lemon. Strain it and when cold add the juice of three and a half lemons and the whites of two eggs well beaten. When it begins to settle whisk it till it becomes white and the consistency of spunge – wet the mould and put it in. Orange made the same way, the yolk of an egg gives it a beautiful colour.

From Miss Clark of Belford Hall's Recipe Book

Lobster a la Braize

Take the meat of one large lobster two ozs of butter, 2 ozs grated bread, beat it all in a mortar with the yolk of an egg, and form it into the shape of a lobster on a plate. Bruise the coral of the lobster and put over it – garnish it with the horns, tail and claws, season with mace, nutmeg, pepper and salt when mixing.

From Mrs Smith's cook (Budle)

Visitors since March 22nd 1821

Mrs Turnbull

Mrs Joplin

Mrs Thompson

Mr G Thompson – Mindrum

Mr Turnbull – Lempitlaw

Mr Sanderson – Cornhill

Mr N Weatherly – Belford

Miss Thomson – Coldstream

Lt Col Werge – Belford

Mrs Werge

Mrs Dodson

Mrs F Compton – Learmouth

Miss Compton

Miss Lawson

Mr Thomson – Scremerston

Dr McColmach

Dr McDonald

Mrs McDonald

Mr Turnbull – Seamer

Mrs Turnbull

Mr Turnbull – Crookes

Mr Leitch – Hirsel

Mr Thompson – Dunse

Mr Fenwick Compton

Mr James Thomson

Mrs Adam Johnston

Miss Darling – Melkington

2 Miss Comptons

Revd. Thompson – Belford

Major Dunlop

Mr Dickson – Belchester

Mr Pringle

Mr Harrowgate

Mr Wm Manderson – Humbleton

Mrs Thomson – Oxenridge

Mr Thomson

Miss E Thomson

Mr Adam Thomson – Dunse

Mr Allan – Ford

Miss Thomson – Oxenridge

Revd. Mr Hume – Yetholm

Revd. Mr Stark

Mr Scott – Coldstream

Mr Turnbull – Dunbar

Mr Turnbull – Portobello

Mr Turnbull – Eastfield

Mr Douglas – Coldstream

Mrs Douglas

Mr Mir

Mrs Mir

Mrs J Mir

Miss Pinkerton

Mr Lawson

Mr Downing

Rev R Scott

Miss Grayson

Mr R Manderson – Cornhill

Mr Edward Smith

Mrs Sanderson – Humbleton

Miss Sanderson

Mr J Rennie – Phantasie

Mr Smith – Fireburn

Miss Smith

Mr Dixon

Mr Laidler

Mr Hunt

Mr Nicholson – Fowberry

Mr Donaldson – Cheswick

Mr Henderson – Ancroft

Major Jameson – 64th Regt.

Colonel Johnstone – Earshaw

Miss Johnstone

Miss Trotter

Miss Redpath

Mrs Thompson – Mindrum

Revd. Mr Gibb

Mr Furnass

Mrs Furnass

Miss Dixon – Stonefold

Mrs Thomson – Scremerston

Revd Mr Thomson

Mrs Dobson

Mr Cockburn – Outchester

Mr Alder – Morris Hall

Miss Air

Revd. G Cunningham

Mrs Cunningham

Mr Weatherly – Old Cambus

Mr Weatherly – Hoprig

Mr Hood – Chalkielaw

Mr Hood – Path head

Mr Thompson – Pawston

Mrs Thompson

Miss Thompson

The Weatherlys

John Weatherly died in 1807 at the age of 54 and was buried alongside Mary, his wife, in Foulden churchyard. His obituary in the Newcastle Courant described him as an 'honest and worthy man'. In 1805 he had purchased the 'Town Farm' and adjoining cottages in nearby Easington. At the time, the owner of the Belford and Easington estate was eager to sell, so the Easington portion was 'hived off'. John Weatherly was able to buy the farm as an investment for £7,500 with Luke Scott as sitting tenant, until the lease expired in 1811.

James inherited the Easington property together with a cash bequest on his father's death. He continued to farm at Outchester until the lease with the Royal Greenwich Hospital expired in 1811 – when he moved on to farm Budle Hill. At the same time the lease expired on the Easington property and James immediately put it on the market at an asking price of £17,500. Papers concerning the Weatherlys were auctioned by an Alnwick solicitor in 2010 which revealed that James and his brother Nicholas had used their inheritances to speculate in property – they bought the leases of a Brewery in Cannongate and the Beehive public house, together with the tenancy of Stonyhill farm, all in Alnwick.

It would appear, however, that these speculations were made before transactions for Easington had begun, and an increasingly desperate James agreed to a sale of Easington for only £11,500 – but all too late. The completion for the farm dragged on and James and Nicholas were declared bankrupts in 1811.

In 1813 James married Catherine Wilson of Alnwick, seemingly settling to farm at Budle and raising five children over the next few years. By 1825, however, he decided on a career change and advertised his services as an auctioneer in the Newcastle Courant. It would appear he continued to live at Budle Hill, but at some point the farm was taken over by James and Young Weatherly, second cousins from Link Hall - when it was put up for sale in January 1837 it was noted as being 'in the occupation' of Messrs Weatherly. Whether James senior was in residence is not known.

Then something happened which was to change their lives.

The Berwick Advertiser 29th April 1837

Suicide – on Sunday morning last the body of Mr Weatherly of Budle was found suspended from a tree on a neighbouring plantation. The unfortunate gentleman had gone from home on Friday morning, and not having returned by night, a search was made for him at the adjoining farms, but no trace of him could be discovered at that time.

Initially this was thought perhaps to be Eleanor's brother – until a notice in the Newcastle Courant announced the death of James Weatherly, late of Outchester in Edinburgh in 1853. Both the 1841 and 1851 census list James and Catherine living in the city with their children. Obviously he had fled there following the suicide of his cousin – at that time suicide was a criminal offence, and would have brought considerable disgrace upon the family.

Nicholas was serving his apprenticeship as a Land surveyor when his father died. At the time, he was living in Hornsingham in Wilshire, and possibly employed on the Longleat estate. He was to inherit £3,500 when the Outchester lease expired, but meanwhile was to be kept in a 'full and affluent manner' and paid £50 a year for 'cloathes and other necessaries'. On returning north he went into partnership with his brother and, despite being declared bankrupt, somehow his reputation survived. When William Clark bought the Belford estate in 1810, Nicholas surveyed the town of Belford for him, and during the Dobson rebuild of Belford church in 1828, Nicholas was appointed secretary and treasurer for the project.

At the age of 35 he married Isabella Cockburn (formerly of London) in Dunbar – they had just one son. He disappears abruptly from the local scene after 1837; possibly the family suicide marked the end of his career in the area. His house, Belford Villa, was put up for sale and he moved to Newcastle. Shortly afterwards his wife died; yet again he was in financial difficulties. Eventually his son joined him there, taking a post as a draughtsman with the Armstrong factory. Nicholas died in 1854.

Despite their father's careful approach to money and his determination to leave his family well provided for – within a few years his sons had squandered their inheritance.

Susan it seems in her father's eyes, was not to be trusted with money – having had from him 'four hundred pounds or thereabouts'. She was to inherit a thousand pounds on marriage and a further thousand pounds in trust after her death for her lawful children. Despite her surprising engagement, she did not marry Mr Smith after all. In 1808 she married George Turnbull, a doctor from Dunbar. In the diary, Eleanor mentions Dr Turnbull as an occasional visitor to Outchester, although he was never classed as a 'beau' and there was no hint of romance towards either sister. Susan of course moved to Dunbar, she and George had seven children – two sons became doctors, continuing the medical tradition in Dunbar, another studied dentistry and moved to Manchester, Nicholas the youngest became a proprietor of a boy's school in Brighton. Susan survived her husband by thirty years and died in her eightieth year.

Eleanor inherited £2,400 when she reached 25 or married, which might have made her a sought after bride, but not so. Perhaps the behaviour and financial difficulties of her brothers damaged her marriage prospects. The anticipated marriage to John Younghusband did not materialise. After Outchester was given up and James married, it is likely that she and Nicholas set up home together in Belford.

In 1821 the Berwick Advertiser reported

> *Marriage – On March 21st at Dunbar, Matthew Turnbull, surgeon to Miss Eleanor Weatherly, eldest daughter of Mr John Weatherly Esq. of Easington.*

> *A large number of their friends were at the Kings Arms, Berwick to welcome their arrival, where the day was spent in the most convivial manner. The happy pair in the evening set off for Coldstream.*

Although the register states that Eleanor was of the parish of Belford, it seems likely that she chose to be married from the home of her sister. Matthew was a native of East Lothian, baptised at Yester in 1791, and a relative of George Turnbull. They had obviously first met at Susan's wedding in 1808, although at the time a worldly young woman such as Eleanor was probably not romantically inclined towards a seventeen year old medical student. They made their home in Coldstream where Matthew had his practice. Some five years later Eleanor gave birth to their son Matthew James.

Although there were no more diaries, Eleanor did keep a 'Scriptiana' for the rest of her life. She made notes of recipes and household hints and encouraged her acquaintances to record poetry and prose of their choice. After her marriage she added the names of the people who visited her in Coldstream.

A school for boys, 'Henderson's Academy' was next door to her home on the High Street, and according to the 1841 census, the son of Nicholas and three of Susan's boys were studying there.

Eleanor died in February 1841 aged 56, 'esteemed, regretted and respected by a large circle of friends'. Her son was just 15 and already studying medicine at Edinburgh University. Some 18 months later his father married a doctor's daughter from Dunbar and, in retirement, moved to Belhaven.

Berwick Advertiser April 1866

> *Obituary – The late Dr Turnbull: The remains of M Turnbull who died on Thursday at Belhaven were on Tuesday brought for interment to Lennel churchyard near Coldstream. For half a century Dr Turnbull had practised in this town with very great skill, devotedness and success, giving full satisfaction to his many patients and their friends, and gaining in a rare degree the confidence of the public. The sphere of his professional labours was extensive and they were often of a burdensome and exhaustive description: but he had more than the requisite zeal and energy, along with an admirable promptitude for critical cases, though these qualities were associated with a peculiarly dignified and quiet demeanour. His few words gently, but decisively, secured obedience, and he was equally sparing of drugs.*
>
> *A few years ago he sought a richly earned repose for the evening of his life, and removed to Belhaven, leaving his large and growing practice in the hands of an accomplished son; yet that he was not forgotten in the scene of his fifty years toiling, is proved by the sad sensation with which the inhabitants of Coldstream heard of his death and witnessed on Tuesday, the last honours paid to his remains. His life was marked by a deep but unostentatious piety. For many years Dr Turnbull had been a staff-surgeon in the Berwickshire Militia.*

After qualifying in Edinburgh, Matthew James worked alongside his father in Coldstream and took over the practice when his father retired. He became a magistrate and was appointed JP for Berwickshire, and fittingly for someone living on the bank of the Tweed, a keen fisherman.

He married three times but nevertheless died a childless widower in 1894 – leaving no direct descendants of Eleanor Weatherly.

According to the obituary which appeared in the Scotsman, he was a larger than life figure –

> *A man of striking presence and strongly marked individuality, a genial manner which was expressed in ready wit. He dispensed the most liberal hospitality at his board and was a most punctual man – his habits of punctuality amounting almost to eccentricity. By his death, perhaps the best known figure in that part of the country has been removed.*

Also reported at the time of his death -

TREATMENT OF OBESITY

> *The treatment of obesity is often a troublesome task says the Medical Times, chiefly because our patients will not faithfully and perseveringly follow our advice. Dr Turnbull of Coldstream, N.B., whose death is just announced, was a person of great weight, not only as a physician, but as a man. In 1889 he scaled 22st. Finding his condition getting steadily more ponderous, he put himself on a strictly regulated diet with satisfactory results. As his experience may be useful to others, I give it in his own words – 'I breakfasted' he wrote in 1890, 'at nine as usual; took an egg, half a slice of toast, and a small cup of tea. At two, I had a small basin of soup with a piece of toast. Dinner was at eight, when I had a little fish, the wing of a chicken, or an equivalent in mutton with some green vegetables, and a very small bit of cheese with biscuit. After dinner I had half a glass of whiskey in half a tumbler of water, and one cigar; partook of no soup or pudding of any kind with dinner. Under this system I steadily lost weight, so that on December 5th last I found that I weighed 17st 10lb. I gave up drinking any fluid during the day, and my weight at present*

(in the middle of September 1890) is 15st 7lb; thus I have lost in the course of 15 months 6st 7lb.

In the graveyard at Lennel near Coldstream, there is a headstone in memory of Eleanor, Matthew and their son Matthew James. The three wives, Janet, Sophia and Jane are remembered on an obelisk nearby.

His will was long and detailed, yielding a wealth of personal information. Most intriguing bequests included 'a picture of my mother in her Riding Habit', 'a photograph of my father in uniform' and 'an old fashioned chair with work sewn upon it by my mother' – sadly now probably lost. He bequeathed his books to Robert Oliver, the brother of his second wife, previously Sophia Oliver of Lochside House. As a result, the diary had been in the possession of the Oliver family since 1894, and whilst the family certainly knew of the marriage between their ancestor and Doctor Turnbull, they had no idea that the diarist, Eleanor Weatherly was his mother.

The present diary owner, Elspeth Orrom, who inherited the diary from her mother, is the great, great niece of Sophia Oliver and related by marriage to Eleanor.

At the beginning of her diary Eleanor wrote 'should curiosity induce any person to look at this book, I hope they will forgive repetitions'. Never could she have imagined that some 200 years later, her diary would attract so much attention and reach such a wide audience. What began as a simple exercise to improve her handwriting has provided a fascinating social commentary and glimpse of life in north Northumberland at the beginning of the 19th century.

Debts due from the late John Weatherly 10 June 1807.

		£		
Arch.d Mack	Belford	700	–	–
Executors of the late Phil.p Watson		1000	–	–
Ann Richardson	Whittingham	100	–	–
Jos.h Crea surgeon	D.o	300	–	–
David Weatherly	Redheugh	506	16	4
Tho.s Henderson	Belford	100	–	–
Tho.s Hall	Grange Mill	100	–	–
Greenwich Hospital ½ yr.s Rent		296	–	–
D.o	Tythe	80	–	–
John Dunning	Newlands	350	–	–
Property Tax and Leepes		70	–	–
M.r Weddell	Mousen	20	–	–
Sundry persons / small Sums /		100	–	–
Discharged and cancelled		£3722	16	4
John Scott Belford / not paid /		700	–	–
Charged by Will		Debts 4422	16	4
Eleanor Weatherly 2400 – –		Assets 3320	7	–
Susan Weatherly 2400 – –		£1102	9	4
Rich.d Weatherly 3500 – – 8300 – –				
Remains for Ja.s Weatherly 3200 – –				
The supposed Value of Estate £11500 – –				

11: A record of the debts of John Weatherly on his death in 1807, showing the final value of the estate

12: Eleanor's son, Matthew James

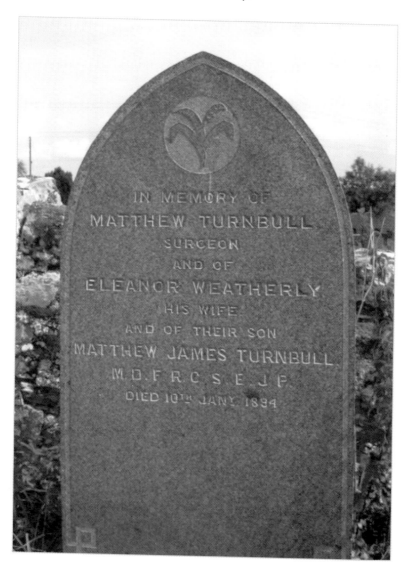

13: Eleanor's headstone

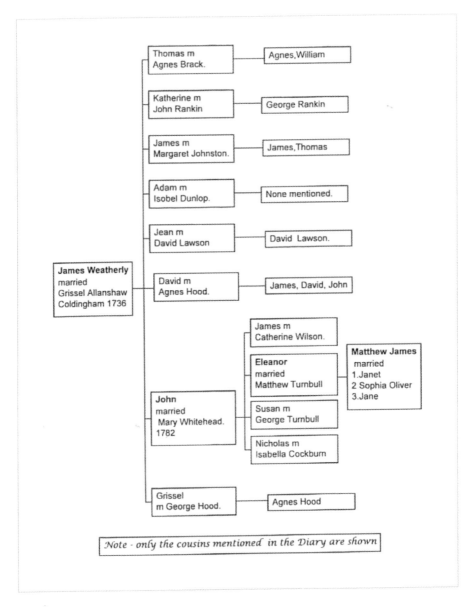

Note - only the cousins mentioned in the Diary are shown

14: The Weatherlys

Glossary of Names

Barber;

Mrs, probably Mary, the widow of Henry Barber who died in 1790. He was variously listed as brewer, farmer and agent for the Belford and Easington estate, previous occupier of West Hall. The mention possibly may have been of Elizabeth wife of Henry junior, they married in 1803. Anthony and Jemima were the children of Henry and Mary. The relatives at Doddington, John and his wife Dorothy (nee Fawcus), were cousins of Eleanor.

Bowlt;

Reverend Andrew, the vicar of Bamburgh, later changed his name to Sharp on his marriage to the niece of Archdeacon Sharp. As the wits of the day remarked 'he bolted into church and came out sharp'.

Brayson;

Jemima, a cousin, daughter of Barbara Whitehead, a sister of Eleanor's mother.

Bromfield;

Mrs, the wife of either James, a linen weaver, or Robert, a merchant.

Burrell;

Nicholas, Joseph and Nelly were cousins, the children of Eleanor Whitehead who was a sister of Eleanor's mother. Nicholas lived at Bassington near Alnwick.

Compton;

Fenwick, a farmer of Learmouth who married Mary Younghusband in 1804.

Dinning;

John, tenant of Newlands. After the death of Henry Barber he became agent for the Belford and Easington Estate. He and his wife Frances are always referred to as Mr and Mrs Dinning; she died in 1813 and he in 1819, both buried at Lucker. Their daughters were Eleanor's closest friends.

Mary, usually described as Miss Dinning, married Alexander Thomson in 1812. He (Sandy) and his sister Betsy are mentioned in the diary; he farmed at Scremerston near Berwick.

Barbara, her younger sister married Gerard Selby in 1815. He was a solicitor in Alnwick and son of Prideaux Selby, the noted naturalist of Twizel House. Barbara and Gerard are buried at Belford.

Harry (Henry), married Grace Rennie of Linton in East Lothian in 1818. They lived for a while at Newlands and later moved to Broomhouse farm south of Scremerston. Both are buried in the family plot at Lucker.

Goodwill;

Reverend George, the vicar of Belford until his death in 1803. His widow and daughter moved to Berwick.

Humble;

Captain John, of West Hall, married Sarah Bawtree of St Osyth in Essex, which probably accounts for her relative and namesake appearing in the diary.

William, farmer of Bamburgh Friars, married Jane, daughter of the Reverend Maughan.

Maughan;

Reverend Michael, he retired to Bamburgh and occasionally officiated there. He was previously the vicar of Whittingham, also Beadnell.

MacDonald;

Mr Charles of the Bluebell Inn. Reputedly 'fond of the drink' he died in 1799 when the tenancy passed to his wife – the establishment continued to be known by her husband's name. Charlotte, John and Charles were their children.

Mole;

Joseph and William were brothers who farmed at Easington Grange. William disappears from the diary without comment. Joseph later moved away and is believed to have farmed at Hetton near Lowick.

Perigle;

Reverend Charles was the vicar of Ellingham for over 50 years. Lewis was his brother.

Richardson;

George, he was described elsewhere as an accountant living at Spindleston, possibly with some business interest at the local corn mills (although work did not appear to be one of his priorities). He married Mary Mather who was living at Waren House. She may have been a governess to the Watson family, as they were witnesses to the wedding.

Smith;

Grieve – he married Eleanor Culley a daughter of one of the famed Northumberland agriculturalists. He bought Waren House and eventually owned the entire Budle Estate.

Watson;

Watson and Son, known as William the elder and William the younger, were the owners of Corn Mills at Waren and Spindleston, also of a brewery in Alnwick. Declared bankrupts in 1811, they then retired to Adderstone. Their property interests were later snapped up by the two Weatherly brothers and Grieve Smith.

Chatto moved to London and became a wine and spirit merchant – he was declared bankrupt in 1814 and died shortly afterwards.

Mrs Cap't Watson was previously Dorothea Henrietta Grey, daughter of Henry Grey of Shoreston. She was the widow of John Watson, a brother of William junior, who died shortly after their marriage in 1799, leaving her with a young son.

John, who Eleanor recounts at one time as being 'very ill' became a captain in the Army, he married Mary Moffat and settled in Ireland.

Joseph died in 1806, aged 17.

Yellowly joined the Bengal Infantry, and died in India in 1818.

Margaret remained unmarried and lived in Belford until her death in 1825.

William, became a lawyer. He married Elizabeth Howard of St Oysth in Essex, lived there and then in Tredegar Square in London, died in 1864.

Werge;

Miss, a relative of the Younghusbands, John Werge of Horton Castle near Chatton married a Margaret Younghusband in 1760. Miss Werge was probably his granddaughter.

Whitehead;

Mary, although not mentioned in the diary, was the wife of John Weatherly and mother of James, Eleanor, Susan and Nicholas.

Her sister, Eleanor Whitehead, married George Burrell of the parish of Eglingham.

Wood;

The family were cousins of the Younghusbands. Thomas Younghusband of the parish of Chatton married Mary Wood of Carham. Thomas and Mary later moved to Elwick.

Yellowly;

Adam, the unmarried brother of Mrs Dorothy Watson, the wife of William the younger of Waren House.

Young;

Mr and Miss of Newham Newhouses – not identified, although Isabella Young of Newham married William Weatherly of Dunbar in 1798 and moved to Link Hall in 1804.

Younghusband;

The branch at Elwick were considered the 'younger branch' of an old Northumbrian family, the children of Thomas and Mary.

George, despite his 'flirtation' with Barbara Dinning, married Maria Astley of Cheshire in 1806. He served with the 3rd Dragoons and the Spanish service, and died at Santander in 1834.

John Wood, married Eliza Dean, daughter of a Lancashire clergyman, in 1818. He continued to live and farm at Elwick until his death in 1846. He was buried at Bamburgh.

Margaret, married Parke Pittar of Calcutta, an East India Company merchant (Silversmiths) in 1816; she died in 1826.

Mary (usually called Miss), married Fenwick Compton of Carham in 1804, lived at Learmouth. She remained in touch with Eleanor and visited her in Coldstream, died in 1835.

Oswald, the eldest son, married Elizabeth Younghusband of Tuggal Hall in 1799, farmed at Ross until his death in 1828.

Robert, corresponded with Eleanor whilst serving in Dublin. He married Catherine Robertson, widow of a captain in the Bengal Artillery. Served as an Army major, one time occupant of Middleton Hall; died in 1853 at Alnwick.

William, married Anne Younghusband of Tuggal Hall in London in 1806. A Commander with the Hon. East India Company Service, believed to have held property in Beadnell, died in 1846.

***

Note: The Younghusbands, Werges, Woods and Comptons were all related through the marriages of their ancestors.

It was the custom for the older generation of men to be addressed as Mr – married women of all ages were addressed as Mrs or by their husband's name – an elder daughter was addressed as Miss (for example Miss Dinning and Miss Barbara Dinning). First names were commonly used, however, for younger male acquaintances (beaux).

Sources

Bibliography:

Bowen Jane – Of Roads, Posts and Coaches; *from Further Aspects of Belford 2011; Published by Belford Bowen Publishing.*

Clarke David V – The History of the Belford United Reformed Church 1976.

Cleland Elizabeth – A New and Easy Method of Cookery 1755; *Re-published jointly by the Paxton Trust/Prospect Books 2005.*

Good James – Directory of Berwick upon Tweed 1806; *Produced by Berwick History Society 1999.*

Taylor Elizabeth – The Art of Cookery 1769; *Produced by Berwick History Society 2002.*

The Weatherly Papers, private.

Newspapers; Periodicals:

Berwick Advertiser, Haddingtonshire Courier, London Gazette, Newcastle Courant.

Monthly Mirror – The Stage - Vol 19 1805.

Records consulted at:

Berwick upon Tweed Record Office.

Durham University Library, Special Collections.

East Lothian Archives and Local History Centre.

Northumberland Collections Service, Woodhorn.

Websites:

North East Inheritance Database (pre 1858 Probate Records).

http:www.familyrecords.durham.ac.uk

Census returns, England.

http:www.findmypast.co.uk

Parish records, Census returns, Wills and Testaments, Scotland.

http:www.scotlandspeople.gov.uk

Wanney Books is a local publisher, based in Alnwick. We are aiming to create a range of books that celebrate the history, culture and landscape of Northumberland.

For our current books please visit our website at

www.wildsofwanney.co.uk

We want to help local authors get their ideas for books about Northumberland into print. If you have a project that you would like to discuss, please get in touch at

books@wildsofwanney.co.uk

We would also welcome any ideas for new book titles.